Update democracy !!!

A pledge for awareness and action

Christian Jelen

Update democracy!!! A pledge for awareness and action

Paperback black & white: ISBN 9798227849717

ENQUIRIES: cb@jayceee.com

Foreword

Over the past few years, I have experienced a sense of power-lessness while observing the challenges democratic societies face globally. As my concerns deepened, I took the initiative to engage in some reading and research, gathering information I could then discuss with friends in person and online. I noticed that discussions and information about democracy were usually limited to academics and their presentations. This has fuelled a genuine desire to share and exchange ideas based on my research, motivating me to write and illustrate this book. I especially feel passionate about the need to present and discuss these questions in an accessible way and with the younger generation. The book tries to do three things:

-Explain vital elements of a democratic society

-Give an update on the state of democracy in the world and the challenges it faces

-Motivate and encourage the pursuit of a more democratic world.

In a world grappling with pressing issues such as global warming, I think it's crucial that we must unite to revitalise democracy. I trust that this book will ignite your inspiration to explore ideas that could shape its future. The book also includes some questions I keep asking myself. Maybe you are interested in asking them yourself and trying to find some answers.

We are all part of a community of activists who have existed long before us and will continue long after we are gone, on the slow, gradual path to enlightenment.

Christian Jelen

Contents

2. The economy and democracy

2.1 Wealth accumulation and democracy

2.2 Basic economic concepts

2.3 The Economy Gone Wrong

2.4 Social capital

3. Recognising dictatorship

3.1 Legitimate politician or dictator?

5.4 10 strategies of mind manipulation

5.5 Using violence

5.6 Stories help privileged groups stay in power

5.7 Extremist stories

6. New foundations for a democracy

7.1 Be the change you want to see: we must start with ourselves

6.2 Triggering change in social interaction with others

6.3 Creating the technological infrastructure for change

7.3 The arts and democracy

8. Anti-corruption strategies

9. Upcoming challenges

10. Organising system change

Precious people

There are many funny, weird, very precious beings on this planet. We are usually good-hearted and quite intelligent. On our best days, we think, while being different, that we are all worth the same. Democracy has proven to be the most beneficial system for us to live together. Pluralism is about appreciating our differences in society, like beliefs, cultures, and interests. It means understanding that people have different views and goals, and it's essential to respect these differences. In politics, pluralism means there are many groups with different ideas, all trying to influence government decisions. They compete fairly to make their voices heard. Pluralistic societies have ways for everyone to speak up, like free speech and democratic processes. Pluralism strengthens democratic societies by encouraging discussion, tolerance, and compromise. It shows that having different opinions enriches society and helps make better decisions for everyone.

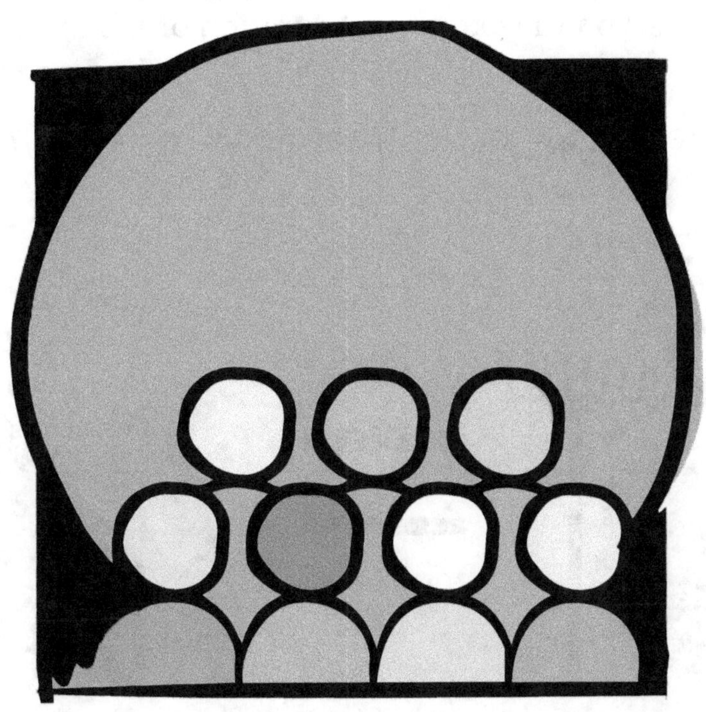

A citizen is a person who, by place of birth, naturalisation or nationality of one or both parents, is granted full rights and responsibilities as a community member. Everyone should have an equal chance to impact decisions that affect fellow citizens. Our idea of democracy is often: "Democracy is great when everything in society is organised the way I like it." But to make democracy happen, the question is probably more: "Can I endure not living the life I want because of the needs of others?" I think a beautiful, natural, and harmonious democracy is one of closeness, compassion, and curiosity.

Interesting fact

In the German constitution, the "forfeiture" (meaning loss) of fundamental rights means that those rights can be withdrawn from anyone who "abuses them to fight against the free, democratic basic order." The Bundestag (parliament), the federal government or a state government can apply for forfeiture of fundamental rights. In this case, the Federal Constitutional Court decides on the extent and duration of the forfeiture.

Universalism: equal treatment for everyone

Being accountable means taking responsibility for your actions, decisions, and their consequences. It involves being answerable for your behaviour, both to yourself and to others. When you're accountable, you acknowledge your role in a situation, whether positive or negative, and you're willing to accept the consequences, learn from them, and make necessary adjustments. Accountability is essential in personal and professional settings as it fosters trust, integrity, and reliability. In a "universalist" society, the goal of an accountable and fair government is the welfare and happiness of equal citizens. Citizens expect that public goods are distributed equally and fairly as a norm. Laws are enforced uniformly for everyone. Every citizen not only has the theoretical freedom to pursue their desires but also practical freedom to access essentials like education and healthcare. It's freedom for all, not just for some.

Particularism: privileged groups are treated better

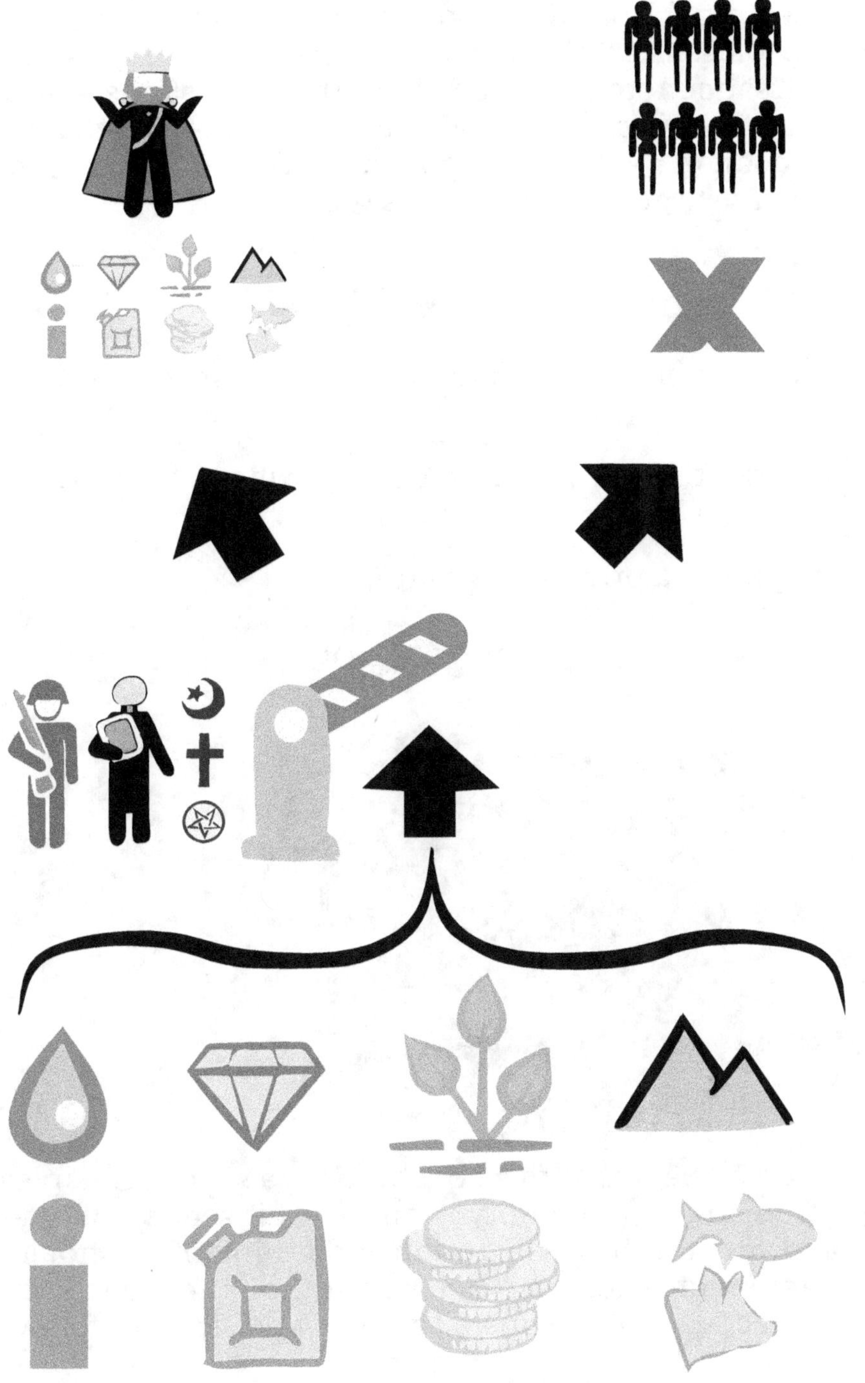

In a "particularist" society, privileged groups have greater access to public goods and often operate above the law. The ideal scenario for privileged groups is when unequal treatment becomes normal behaviour, with citizens only expecting similar treatment to everybody with the same status. We are taught that privilege is natural. We are never taught that there is a connection between our poverty and their wealth. I think a particularist society is not a true democracy.

What do you think?

Are you living in a particularist or universalist country?

Can you identify any privileged groups where you live?

Are you part of a privileged group?

Constitution

A democracy begins with a constitution, a set of principles that guide how a community is run. The citizens should design and vote for the constitution and I think there should be a referendum each time the constitution is changed. It's an ethical code that members agree on and strive to follow.

16

These principles include laws, how authority is shared, government responsibilities, and the rights guaranteed to the citizens within the community. It can also include other details such as limiting how much debt the government is allowed to create. The Constitution also protects us from ourselves: not being able to reintroduce the death penalty, for example.

What do you think?

Some constitutions allow the fundamental rights of citizens to be taken away: is this good for a democracy?

Can you think of movements or organisations that have hatred or bias so embedded in them that they threaten democracy?

The duties and rights of the citizen are defined in the constitution.

It's natural for us to desire human rights and individual freedom. I think the constitution should ensure freedom of faith, conscience, artistic and scientific expression, and the right to assemble. It should also set boundaries on what a government can enforce on its citizens. Citizens have freedom of choice, freedom to act independently, and freedom to pursue self-interest activities (within the law). From a community-focused viewpoint, citizens have duties and responsibilities towards society. Duties required by law are to pay taxes, defend the nation, serve in court, attend school, and obey the law. The responsibilities of citizens are to inform and educate themselves, be active members of the democratic society, and make the government accountable. I think citizens should be involved in community services and promote the common good.

What do you think?

Do you think the constitution's unwritten or partially written aspects can create confusion about laws, making them open to different interpretations? Can this lack of clarity weaken the stability and effectiveness of the government and legal system?

Should religious law be identical to civil law?

Do you think that sometimes shared goals are more important than individual needs?

How would you like to participate in a democratic society?

Interesting facts: Countries and their "constitutions"

United Kingdom: The United Kingdom has an unwritten constitution based on various disconnected laws.

New Zealand: New Zealand has an unwritten constitution that relies on statutes, constitutional conventions, and the Treaty of Waitangi.

Israel: Israel does not have a formal, written constitution. Instead, its constitutional framework is based on laws, statutes, and legal conventions.

Saudi Arabia: Saudi Arabia does not have a codified constitution. Instead, it relies on the Quran and the Sunnah (traditions of the Prophet Muhammad) as fundamental legal sources, along with royal decrees and laws.

Canada: Canada has a partially written constitution, with some elements codified in the Constitution Acts of 1867 and 1982. However, other constitutional principles are derived from conventions and unwritten sources.

Sweden: Sweden has a partially unwritten constitution, with some constitutional principles found in statutes and laws, while others are based on conventions and historical practices.

Norway: Norway's constitution is partially written, with critical elements found in the Constitution of Norway, but it also relies on conventions and statutes.

Netherlands: The Netherlands has a constitutional monarchy with an unwritten constitution that includes legal statutes and conventions. A constitutional monarchy is a form of government in which a monarch (a king, queen, emperor, or empress) acts as the head of state usually within the parameters of a constitution.

Australia: Australia has a federal constitution, but it is a combination of written and unwritten elements. Some constitutional conventions and practices are not explicitly outlined in the written Constitution.

Oman: Oman does not have a formal, written constitution. The Basic Statute of the State serves as a constitutional document, and the legal system is influenced by Islamic law.

"Old school" democracy

In most democracies, a government is elected for a limited time and consists of three branches:

1. Legislative: makes laws and the constitution

2. Executive: carries out laws (president, cabinet, public servants)

3. Judicial: evaluates laws (courts)

The actions and budgets of the three branches should be transparent to the citizens.

What do you think?

Is it essential that individuals in the three branches, including judges and lawmakers, are elected in a democratic process and are not nominated by privileged groups?

An accountable government

Overall, an accountable government fosters trust among its citizens, promotes good governance, and contributes to society's overall well-being. I think those in power, whether elected officials or public servants, should be held responsible for their conduct and the consequences of their decisions. Key aspects of an accountable government include:

Transparency allows citizens to understand how and why decisions are made. An accountable government provides clear and accessible information about its actions, policies, and decision-making processes.

Responsiveness: An accountable government listens to its citizens' concerns and feedback. It addresses grievances, takes appropriate action, and adjusts policies when necessary in response to the public's needs and expectations.

Rule of law: An accountable government adheres to the rule of law, ensuring its actions are consistent with legal frameworks.

Independent oversight and checks: Accountability involves mechanisms for oversight and checks on the government's power. This can include independent institutions, such as an ombudsman (an individual used to investigate complaints), the judiciary, or legislative bodies that monitor and scrutinise government actions to prevent abuse of power.

Electoral accountability: In democracies, elected officials are accountable to the electorate. Through regular elections, citizens can evaluate the government's performance and decide whether to retain or replace those in power.

Ethical conduct: An accountable government upholds ethical standards in its operations, demonstrating integrity and honesty. This includes addressing issues of corruption and ensuring that public resources are used for the benefit to citizens.

Commitment to fight corruption: Robust institutions, ethical standards, and a commitment to fair and open competition help mitigate the risks associated with favouritism and ensure that decisions are made in the best interests of the broader population rather than a select few.

Controlling abuse of power

Within a constitutional democracy, each branch holds the capacity to modify the actions of the other branches. The three branches of government (executive, legislative, and judicial) are separate and have the power to check each other. This system of checks and balances is designed to prevent any one branch from becoming too powerful – a measure designed to curb corruption and safeguard us from rulers driven by an insatiable thirst for power.

I think laws ought to be crafted to fulfil citizens' fundamental needs, including access to food, healthcare, education, and the promotion of an ethical society. These laws should be founded on the principle that each citizen has the right to pursue happiness regardless of wealth. When these laws fall short of achieving these objectives, they must undergo revision.

What do you think?

Are there any laws in your country that need revising?

1.2 Decision-making

In any group of people, you get some who are vocal and some who are quiet. Often, the vocal individuals end up leading the group. At first, the quiet people let the vocal people get their way. They don't like confrontations and often they don't care.

But the quiet people have opinions too. And the longer they need to listen to loud people's opinions and witness decisions being made without their own input, the more likely things in a group stop working:

-quiet people have knowledge and ideas that could contribute to finding solutions, but if they are not getting heard, the group as a whole is missing out on finding solutions

-quiet people get frustrated and dig their heels in, slowing down whatever the group is trying to achieve.

That's true for your family, sports club, town council, country, even the planet. This is why it's so crucial to establish a democratic decision-making process.

Represent and organise! Political vacuum is often quickly filled with democracy abusers.

A political vacuum refers to a situation with an absence or breakdown of effective governance or leadership within a specific political system or geographical area. This absence of authority or leadership can occur for various reasons, such as government instability, the collapse of existing political structures, or a failure to establish new ones. Leaders naturally emerge within any group, often holding power without being held accountable. When power shifts, frequently, someone else will step in, possibly less qualified and not with good intentions. Therefore, it's vital to establish fair and transparent methods for choosing and replacing leaders and to agree on our organisational structure. Representation is at the heart of democracy, and those chosen to represent the people must be ready to fulfil their roles and improve the situation. Representation in a democracy refers to the principle that citizens are represented by elected officials who make decisions on their behalf. In a democratic system, citizens choose their representatives through free and fair elections. These representatives, such as members of parliament or congress, are responsible for voicing the concerns and interests of the people they represent in the government's decision-making process.

Representation ensures that diverse voices and perspectives within society are heard and considered when making laws and policies. It allows for the expression of popular will and enables citizens to participate in the governance of their country indirectly through their elected representatives. Effective representation requires transparency, accountability, and responsiveness from elected officials to the needs and desires of their constituents. Overall, representation is a fundamental aspect of democracy, ensuring that the government remains responsive and accountable to the people it serves.

The road to decision-making: anarchy, authoritarianism and democracy

In an "anarchist society" there is no formal government, laws, or institutions of authority. Instead, individuals or groups organise themselves through voluntary cooperation and mutual aid, often based on principles of decentralisation and self-governance. Anarchism can take various forms, from peaceful and cooperative communities to more radical movements advocating for the abolition of all forms of hierarchical authority, including capitalism and the state. While often associated with chaos or disorder, proponents of anarchism argue that it represents a vision of a more egalitarian and liberated society, where power is decentralised and individuals are free to govern themselves without coercion or oppression.

• 	Power is focused on a single leader or a small group, like a ruling party or military.

• 	Citizens have limited freedom to participate in politics, like voting in fair elections, and may face punishment for disagreeing with the government.

•	There aren't many independent groups that keep the government's power in check, like a free press or courts.

•	The government controls many aspects of society, such as the media and economy, to stay in power.

•	Laws might not always be applied fairly, and citizens might not have many legal rights.

This type of government is different from democracy, where power is shared among different other groups, and people can participate in making decisions. Even though authoritarian governments might promise stability, they often restrict people's freedoms and rights.

Democracy is a form of government that relies on the participation of its citizens to make decisions. It is based on the principles of representation, participation, and decision-making. Democracy requires well-informed and engaged citizens with sound knowledge of the world. It aims to tap into the collective wisdom of its people using the best available tools to ensure the well-being of all. However, democracy is not without its challenges. There are various models for types of democratic systems. Let's look at each in turn.

Deliberative Democracy Model

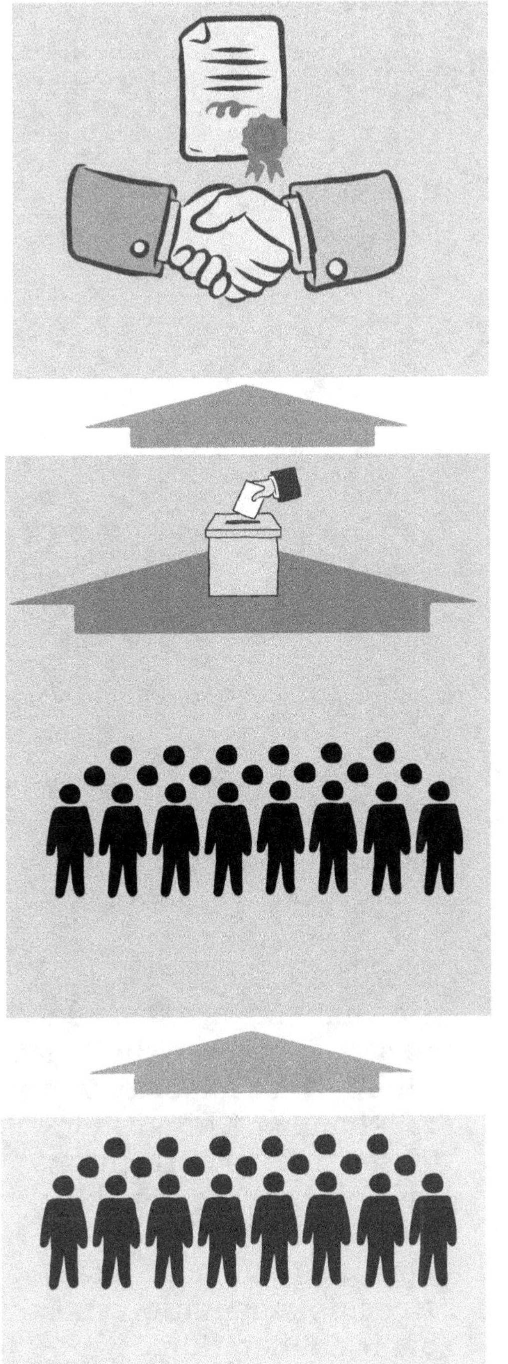

In a deliberative democracy model, individuals both consume and contribute to the formation of policies, ideologies, and information. They meet in public gatherings or online platforms to advocate for and be influenced by ideas, ideologies, and necessities. The benefits encompass granting people an active voice, enabling direct participation, and fostering opportunities for personal growth. I think deliberative democracies emphasise participation, involvement, reasoned discourse and public involvement, aiming to avoid drastic outcomes, like the emergence of anarchy, excessive participation, biassed emphasise reasoned discourse and public participation involvement, aiming to prevent drastic outcomes like the emergence of anarchy, excessive participation, biassed decision-making, and sluggish deliberation. The likelihood of citizens accepting decisions made through this model is also expected to be than or more significant than other decision-making models.

Wise Elite Model

In this model, decision-making is entrusted to a chosen few – the "wise elite" – via a majority voting mechanism. This system poses risks of corruption and bias among the elite. Nevertheless, it offers the advantages of cost-effective implementation and swift deliberation.

Rational Choice Model

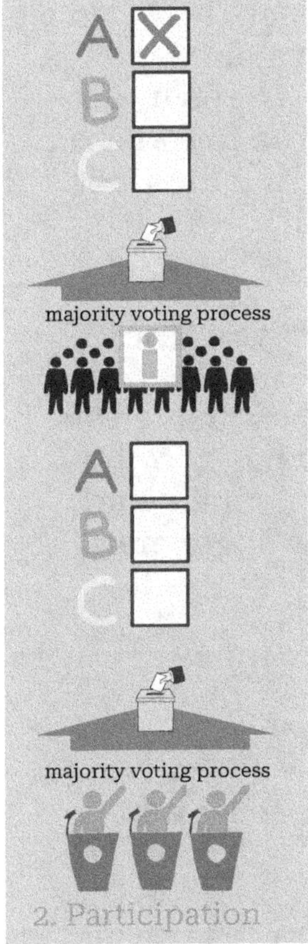

In the rational choice model, people are consumers of policies, ideologies, and information. These are formulated by the state and politicians. The dangers are that people's votes validate the privileged groups' desires; after all, the privileged groups have the resources and propaganda machines to advertise their agenda, while it can be complex and challenging for the people to voice their own needs. Votes for policies are treated as in an economic market, for example, when political parties in a coalition try to form a government and have to compromise on their policies with the opposition.

Non-human model

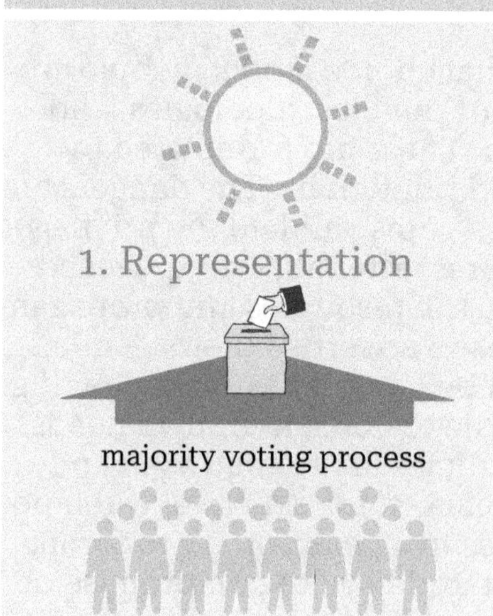

In the past, we were willing to entrust our choices to omens and oracles. Today, are we willing to relinquish control of our lives to artificial intelligence (AI)? Can we consider a system democratic if we lack a deep understanding of the foundations behind the decisions made on our behalf?

What do you think?

Is truth the best guarantee and the only basis for freedom and democracy and relationships in general?

Is democracy the best way to organise society?

Interesting fact

The first article of the Universal Declaration of Human Rights of the United Nations declares: "All human beings are born free and equal in dignity and rights. They are endowed with reason and conscience and should act towards one another in a spirit of brotherhood."

Consensus decision-making

Instead of using a simple majority rule, a group using consensus is committed to reaching agreement among all members. When some citizens strongly oppose a decision that has been made, especially if they feel they haven't been heard, they will drag their feet and cause problems. Solutions that everyone actively supports or at least can live with are much more beneficial for everyone.

What do you think?

How should decisions be made at your sports club, school, or the town you live in?

Who faces the consequences of a bad outcome of a decision?

What should the consequences be for those who decided when something went wrong, in your sports club or country?

Interesting facts:

The availability of voter registers varies from country to country. Some countries make voter registers public, while others do not. For example, in the United States, voter registration information is generally considered public record. Still, in countries like Germany and Canada, voter registers are not publicly accessible due to privacy concerns.

In the UK, some people have suggested that 50 constituency seats should be reserved for MPs aged 18–30. There have also been suggestions to open elections to 16-17 year-olds.

In the current UK voting system (called "first past the post,","" where one party simply has to get a majority of seats to win), thousands of votes are wasted: a candidate can win by three votes or 100,000 votes. The party that wins the most parliamentary seats is not necessarily the party that won the most votes overall. Parties are penalised if their support is spread across the country rather than concentrated in certain areas.

1.3 Problems and dangers of democracies

The value of values in a democracy

Having a well-functioning democracy doesn't always ensure a peaceful society. Even today, in many democracies, like Switzerland, extremist parties can gain popularity. No perfect democracy exists, as democratic systems are inherently human-made and subject to imperfections. However, several countries in the 20th century were considered to have strong democratic foundations, such as the

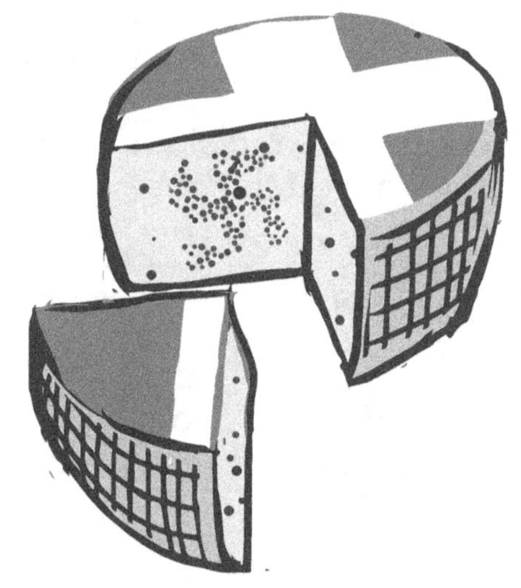

United States, several Western European nations, and others. Each had unique constitutional, legislative, and legal models, but all faced challenges and criticisms. Perfect democracy remains an ideal rather than a realised form of governance.

It's crucial to remember that human qualities such as ethics, compassion, honesty, and wisdom form the foundation of every democracy. Continuous dialogue is necessary because a democracy can swiftly shift from being confident, tolerant, and compassionate to becoming racist and hateful. Have a look at how vulnerable individuals are treated in a society – older people, disabled people, and even animals: how they are being treated is the moral barometer of that society.

What do you think?

Which ethical qualities do we need to cultivate to create a peaceful society?

Religion and state

A government with a solid religious influence is called a theocratic government. It's essential to recognise that the relationship between religion and governance is complex, and not all governments with religious influences exhibit the same drawbacks. Some countries struggle to balance between spiritual and religious values and principles of pluralism, tolerance, and individual rights. Potential and disadvantages might be:

Limited religious freedom: It may restrict the freedom of individuals who adhere to different faiths or hold secular beliefs. Minority religions or non-believers may face discrimination or persecution.

Lack of pluralism: It may suppress political and society's diversity of perspectives and voices and voices in society. This lack of diversity can stifle creativity, innovation, and democratic discourse.

Inequality and discrimination: A theocratic government may enforce laws or policies that discriminate against certain groups based on religious beliefs, gender, or other characteristics. This can lead to social divisions and inequality.

Interference in personal lives: A government strongly influenced by religious doctrines may seek to regulate personal behaviour and lifestyle choices based on religious,spiritual principles. This can intrude into individuals' private lives and limit personal freedoms.

Stifled social progress: Rigidity in religious doctrines may hinder social progress and advancements. Scientific research, technological innovations, and social reforms may be impeded if they conflict with religious teachings or dogma.

Conflict with secularism: Maintaining a separation between religious institutions and the state may be challenging. This can lead to conflicts between religious authorities and secular governance structures.

Resistance to criticism: Governments closely tied to religion may be less tolerant of criticism, dissent, or challenges to religious orthodoxy. This can limit the development of a culture of open debate and free expression.

Potential for authoritarianism: Theocratic governments have the potential to become authoritarian, as religious leaders or institutions may wield significant power without sufficient checks and balances. This concentration of power can lead to abuses and lack of accountability..

Stagnation in education: Religion's strong influence on governance may lead to limitations in educational curricula, focusing on religious teachings at the expense of a well-rounded and comprehensive education. This can affect intellectual development and critical thinking.

What do you think?

Should the three branches be separate from the religious institutions?

Is the state intertwined with religion in the country you live in?

Populism in democracy

Populism is a political style that claims to "represent the interests of the common people against an alleged corrupt elite." It offers simple solutions in a complex world. Here are some dangers associated with populist politicians in a democratic context.

Erosion of institutions:

Populists often criticise and undermine established institutions, such as the judiciary, the media, and other checks and balances. This erosion weakens the democratic system's ability to uphold the rule of law and maintain a separation of powers.

Authoritarian tendencies

They often exhibit authoritarian tendencies by concentrating power in the hands of the executive branch, sidelining other branches of government, and limiting the independence of institutions that serve as checks on executive power.

Divisiveness and polarisation

They typically frame the political discourse in terms of "us versus them, " creating a polarised and divisive political environment. This can hinder constructive dialogue and compromise, essential to a healthy democratic process.

Undermining minority rights: They may target minority groups, using populist rhetoric to marginalise or scapegoat specific segments of the population. This undermines the protection of minority rights, a crucial aspect of a well-functioning democracy.

Short-term policy focus: Populists tend to prioritise short-term policies that appeal to their base but lack a long-term vision or sustainability. This focus on immediate popularity can lead to decisions that neglect broader societal needs or contribute to economic instability.

Anti-intellectualism: They promote anti-intellectual sentiments, dismissing expert opinions, scientific evidence, and traditional sources of knowledge. This can undermine evidence-based policymaking and erode public trust in informed decision-making.

Threat to freedom of the press: They attempt to control or manipulate the media, limiting press freedom and suppressing dissent. An independent and free press is essential for informing the public and holding those in power accountable.

Diminished respect for democratic norms: Populist leaders often disregard established democratic norms and conventions, such as respecting term limits or accepting electoral outcomes. This behaviour weakens the democratic fabric. A populist's tools are Dividing groups of people, using economic insecurity, patriotism, and nationalism. Populists can contribute to a culture of political instability.

Have you ever heard these before?

The Populist's tools are dividing groups of people, using economic insecurity, patriotism, and nationalism. Populists are very good at making people believe in what they say: Hitler made extremism sound like a democratic victory.

"There is 'us'..................... and 'them'

We are the 'haves'..... they are the 'have nots'

Jobs and wealth will
be taken by "them"

We should be
proud of "our" country

"Our" country is better than the rest.

Instability in a democracy

Instability in a democracy can have various detrimental effects on a Nation's political, social, and economic aspects. Addressing and preventing instability in a democracy requires a commitment to effective governance, respect for democratic norms, transparent institutions, and mechanisms for peaceful conflict resolution. Building and maintaining political stability is crucial for fostering a thriving democracy and ensuring the nation's and citizens' well-being. Here are some dangers associated with instability in a democratic system:

Erosion of public trust: Political instability often leads to a loss of confidence in democratic institutions. When citizens perceive that their government to unable cannot maintain stability, trust in the democratic process can diminish, potentially undermining the legitimacy of the entire political system. Political instability, such as social unrest and protests, can contribute to economic uncertainty and negatively impact investment, economic growth, and job creation. Businesses may hesitate to invest in an environment marked by political volatility, potentially leading to economic downturns.

Social unrest: Political instability may lead to social unrest and protests as citizens express dissatisfaction with the government's performance. This unrest can lead to disruptions, violence, and insecurity within society.

Weak governance: Constant leadership changes or frequent political crises can result in weak governance. In such circumstances, governments may need help to implement effective policies, address pressing issues, or provide essential public services.

Impact on the rule of law: Political instability can undermine the rule of law, with potential consequences such as corruption, erosion of civil liberties, and a weakened judicial system. A stable and predictable legal environment is crucial for safeguarding individual rights and maintaining social order.

Foreign policy challenges: Countries facing internal instability may find it difficult to formulate and execute consistent foreign policies. Unpredictable domestic situations can hinder diplomatic efforts and strain international relationships.

Threat to democratic values: Persistent instability may lead to prioritise temptation for strongman rule or authoritarian measures, as some segments of the population may prioritise temptation for strongman rule or authoritarian measures, as some segments the population segments may prioritise order and security over democratic values. This risks the democratic principles of freedom, equality, and political pluralism.

Ineffective policy implementation: Political instability can disrupt the continuity of policies and hinder their successful implementation. Frequent changes in leadership or government composition may result in inconsistent approaches to governance and policy-making.

Undermining social cohesion: Prolonged instability can contribute to social divisions and fostering a sense of national unity and shared identity polarisation may be difficult. When political conflicts become deeply entrenched, fostering a sense of national unity and shared identity may be challenging.

Diminished international standing: Countries experiencing political instability may see a decline in their international standing. This can affect diplomatic relations, international cooperation, and the perception of the country as a reliable partner on the global stage.

Excessively personalised leadership

To keep democracy strong, we must stick to core values like institutional integrity, transparency, and accountability. It's essential to have a balance between strong leadership and the democratic system's checks and balances to avoid problems linked with overly personalised leadership. Here are some issues that come with too much focus on one person's leadership:

Erosion of democratic institutions: Excessive personalisation often involves concentrating power in the hands of one individual, weakening the checks and balances provided by democratic institutions such as the judiciary, legislature, and independent regulatory bodies. This might cause democratic norms to weaken and power to concentrate in one leader's hands.

Diminished accountability: When decision-making is highly centralised, there may be limited transparency, and leaders may evade responsibility for failures or controversial decisions.

Undermining the rule of law: Leaders who personalise their authority may undermine the rule of law by disregarding established legal norms and processes. This can lead to arbitrary decision-making and weaken the legal foundations that protect individual rights and liberties.

Reduced policy debate: Excessive personalisation can stifle healthy policy debate and discussion within a democracy. When a leader's personality dominates the political landscape, there is a risk that alternative viewpoints and constructive criticism may be marginalised or suppressed.

Weakened political pluralism: Personalised leadership can weaken political pluralism, as institutions and political parties may become subservient to the leader's preferences. This reduces the diversity of political voices and limits the choices available to the electorate.

Cult of personality: Personalised leadership often leads to developing a cult of personality, where the leader is glorified, and their image becomes central to politics. This can be exploited to manipulate public opinion and discourage dissent.

Vulnerability to authoritarianism: Excessive personalisation raises the risk of a leader becoming autocratic or displaying authoritarian tendencies. Leaders who amass too much power may be tempted to undermine democratic processes and institutions to perpetuate their rule.

Ineffective decision-making: When overly personalised, it may be driven by personal preferences or impulses rather than careful consideration of diverse viewpoints and expert advice. This can lead to hasty and poor policy decisions.

Fragility of governance: Democracies benefit from stable and robust governance structures. Excessively personalised leadership can result in governance that is overly dependent on the leader's abilities and may become fragile when faced with challenges or changes.

Risk of succession issues: If leadership is highly personalised, the transition of power, whether due to elections or other circumstances, may be challenging. The absence of strong institutions to guide transitions can lead to political instability.

What do you think?

Given all these challenging aspects of democracy, would you rather not live in one?

Interesting fact

The number of democracies reached an all-time high of 96 electoral democracies in 2016. In 2022, this number has fallen to 90 countries. (Source: Regimes of the World (RoW) Lührmann/Tannenberg/Lindberg)

2. The economy and democracy

2.1 Wealth accumulation and democracy

Must progress mean mass extinction?

Can we call it "progress" if it makes everybody suffer? Should progress be measured only by economic and technological advancement, or should anything else be considered? The uncontrolled drive for profit has led to enormous suffering and "progress" made at the expense of life on Earth. Uncontrolled economic growth is the tumour killing our planet.

Existential and exchange values

Experiential value is the value that something has to us based on our personal experience of it. Exchange value is the value that something has based on its ability to be exchanged for other goods or services. A hug can hold immense experiential significance, yet would you be willing to purchase one? Unlike items with exchange value, such as buying toilet paper, a hug is devoid of such cold and impersonal value. It's crucial not to confuse the two. Similarly, an experience in nature, like a stroll in a forest, carries significant experiential worth. However, it only acquires exchange value when we fell all the trees and construct a factory. To produce toilet paper. (That was a joke.)

How vital are experiential values for your government?

Interesting fact

The Constitution of the Kingdom of Bhutan includes a unique and notable commitment to promoting happiness. The concept of "Gross National Happiness" (GNH) is enshrined in the constitution as a guiding principle for governance. Bhutan places importance on not only economic development but also on the well-being and happiness of its citizens. The preamble of the Bhutanese Constitution emphasises the desire to create a harmonious and just society. It emphasises the commitment to enhancing people's spiritual, physical, and emotional well-being and improving strengthening. While the term "Gross National Happiness" itself may not be explicitly mentioned in the constitution, the underlying philosophy is incorporated into the constitutional framework to prioritise the holistic development and happiness of the Bhutanese people.

On the flipside, Bhutan has committed ethnic cleansing and human rights abuse, and most of its population lives, and most of its population lives in great poverty. Some have described the GNH as a marketing exercise. I think it is important though that not only economic prosperity but the happiness of the citizens is how we measure the success of our democracy.

Interesting quote

"Human communities and families have always been based on belief in 'priceless' things, such as honour, loyalty, morality and love."

Yuval Noah Harari

Adam Smith was a Scottish economist and philosopher. Some consider him "The Father of Capitalism." He wrote two classic works: The Theory of Moral Sentiments (1759) and An Inquiry into the Nature and Causes of the Wealth of Nations (1776).

Smith introduced the idea of the economy as a 'win-win situation, ' where both parties benefit from each other's success. He argued that we could simultaneously enjoy a larger share of prosperity, your gains being linked to my gains could simultaneously enjoy a larger share of prosperity, with your gains linked to my gains could simultaneously enjoy a larger share of prosperity, with your gains being linked to my gains linked to mine. If I am poor, it negatively impacts you because I can't purchase your products or services. Conversely, if I am wealthy, it benefits you because I can buy from you. Smith challenged the traditional view that wealth and morality were in conflict, suggesting instead that being wealthy equates to being moral. In Smith's perspective, people become rich not by exploiting others, but by contributing to overall prosperity.

2.2 Basic economic concepts

"...money is also the apogee of human tolerance. Money is more open-minded than language, state laws, cultural codes, religious beliefs and social habits. Money is the only trust system created by humans that can bridge almost any cultural gap, and that does not discriminate on the basis of religion, gender, race, age or sexual orientation. Thanks to money, even people who don't know each other and don't trust each other can nevertheless cooperate effectively."

—Yuval Noah Harari

"The fruits of hard work are always sweet" is a myth

The idea that hard work and education will lead to prosperity is consistently only sometimes accurate. In today's standard society, it is difficult for most people to achieve even a basic living standard. I think we need to envision a society in which everyone has the opportunity to thrive.

In an economy without ethical considerations, profits are not gained or distributed fairly. Greed to increase profits bulldozes over anything that might stand in the way. It is a cold, greedy, indifferent murder.

Debt and profit are partners.

There is always someone whose wealth is your debt. Imagine an entrepreneur requests a $1 0000 loan from a banker, with a 10% interest rate amounting to $1000. The banker's total repayment of $11, 000 is due within a year. The entrepreneur

wants to generate a profit that covers not only the loan and interest but also operational expenses– the general costs of running their business. Such loans are a vital component fuelling economic activity, alongside factors like ,entrepreneurs and workers, and resourcefulness of entrepreneurs and workers entrepreneurs and workers determination, discipline, skills, and resourcefulness. The state should never run out of money. The amount of money and debt should always end up being zero.

Interesting fact

In the U.S., banks are allowed to loan $10 for every dollar they possess, which means that 90 percent of all the money in U.S. bank accounts is not covered by actual coins and notes.

The economic system and its players

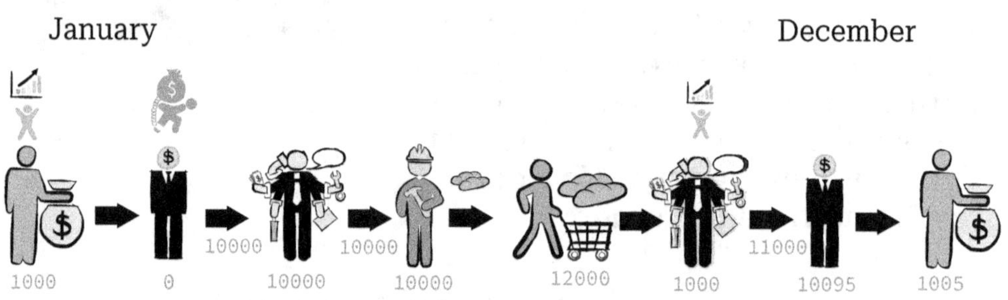

Debt and profit can serve as the driving forces within a society, significantly influencing the functioning of a democracy. Consider the scenario where an entrepreneur, like a baker, secures a loan from a banker.

The entrepreneur wants to produce a product, such as bread, with the assistance of workers. The goal is to generate profit, enabling the entrepreneur to compensate him-/herself, cover the loan interest, and pay their workers. The "consumer" plays a crucial role by purchasing the entrepreneur's products or services, generating profit or benefit for themselves. In this way, consumers actively contribute to profit by buying goods and services.

Recap: An investor gives the banker $1000. The banker provides the entrepreneur $ 10,000, based on a promise that the entrepreneur will pay back $ 10,000, it's a story about $ 9000, based on a promise that the entrepreneur will pay back $ 10,000, plus interest. Our belief in a story creates all our money. In this case, it's a story about $9000—fantasy money made from thin air.

The entrepreneur: slave to debt or swimming in money?

Loans are essential for business-es, as they provide the capital needed to purchase equipment, hire employees, and cover other expenses. Without loans, compa-nies would not be able to produce goods or services, and the econ-omy would halt. However, loans also come with risks. If a business cannot repay its loans, it may be forced to close down, leaving its employees without jobs. Addi-tionally, competition can drive down prices, making it difficult for businesses to profit. As a result, entrepreneurs can find themselves in a precarious po-sition, either saddled with debt or making money while their workers struggle.

The entrepreneur's exchange value

From the perspective of "exchange value" the entrepreneur's primary incentive lies in selling a maximum amount of products at the highest possible price, all while reducing" production costs. Suppose, the en-trepreneur wants to maximise prof-its. In that case, they reinvest profits in production. This motivation can lead to conflicts of interest with the workers, potentially giving rise to unhealthy working conditions and excessive overtime. It can also have adverse environmental effects on the planet. When the cold laws of supply and demand replace human values like empathy, we know we are in trouble.

The workers

Workers constitute the largest segment of citizens, responsible for producing and consuming products and services. When entrepreneurs offer low wages, there can come a time when these wages become too low for the workers to buy the goods themselves when they become too low for the workers to purchase the goods they produce. Wages are low because the rich don't spend much but save. The rich also own machines that do the work, so fewer workers are needed.

The investor

For a limited time, an investor can give a banker money. The banker and investor agree on a specific sum to be paid by the banker, the loan interest rate. When the agreed period ends, investors get their money back, plus the interest earned agreed period comes to an end, investors get their money back, plus the interest earned decided upon for that period.

The banker

The banker gives out loans utilising the investor's money, offering them at a higher loan interest rate than the savings interest rate the investor receives. For the $1 000 received by the investor, the banker is legally allowed to provide a $1 0000 loan. The margin between the higher loan interest and the lower savings interest constitutes the banker's profit - plus the $9 000 the banker created, solely based on

the promise of the entrepreneur. It is crucial for the loan to be backed by a tangible asset with substantial exchange value. This can be the entrepreneurs's money, real estate, property or government bonds. The assets serving as safety for the loan are called the "collateral".

The consumer

A consumer is a citizen who purchases goods and services for personal use. The motivation or non-motivation of a consumer has an impact on working conditions and the sustainability of products and the economy: for example, the consumer has the choice to buy ethically produced products or not.

2.3 The Economy Gone Wrong

Bailing out banks

If an entrepreneur defaults on the loan – that is, fails to pay it back – the banker uses the collateral to cover the debt. Unless there is none in place. When bankers provide unsecured loans (those with no tangible assets to back them up), it sometimes falls upon the government to step in and use the public's funds to bail out these bankers. This situation is reminiscent of a financial crisis, especially when investors request the withdrawal of their deposits.

51

Frequently, the bank lacks the necessary reserves to meet all these demands, resulting in investors losing the funds they entrusted to the bank. Let's recall our example: The banker generated 90% of the loan, essentially "imagined money" based on the entrepreneur's promise. This imaginary money becomes real, regardless of whether the entrepreneur repays it or we, the taxpayers, do. The banker's imaginary money invariably turns into real money.

The government's fiscal responsibility

Fiscal responsibility:

Refers to the practice of managing finances responsibly and sustainably. It involves making prudent spending, borrowing, and saving decisions to ensure long-term financial health and stability.

For governments, fiscal responsibility typically includes:

Balanced Budgets: Ensuring that government spending does not exceed revenue through taxation or borrowing to avoid accumulating excessive debt.

Debt Management: Prudently managing public debt levels

to avoid overburdening future generations with interest payments and to maintain credibility in financial markets.

Efficient Spending: Involves prioritising expenditure on essential services and investments that yield long-term benefits for society while minimising waste and inefficiency.

Revenue Generation: Implementing fair and effective tax policies to generate sufficient revenue to fund public services and investments without burdening taxpayers.

Transparency and Accountability: Providing the public clear and accurate information about government finances and holding government officials accountable for their financial decisions.

Fiscal responsibility is important because it promotes economic stability, encourages investor confidence, and ensures that resources are used efficiently to meet current and future needs. Failure to exercise fiscal responsibility can lead to financial crises, unsustainable debt levels, and negative consequences for governments and the broader economy.

Having to bail out banks in this way reflects a government's inability to regulate the financial market: Inabilities include not enough oversight, weak regulations, lack of transparency, and poorly designed bailout plans. Political meddling, favouritism, or lack of accountability damages public trust. The 2008 financial crisis showed flaws in bailout plans, stressing the need for thorough planning, clear rules, and steps to stop risky behaviour by banks expecting bailouts if they fail. I think the bankruptcy of a bank or corporation should not automatically translate into a nationwide crisis. The government's role is to oversee and enforce laws that safeguard the interests of all citizens, encompassing workers, investors, entrepreneurs, consumers, and bankers.

No recession and a high GDP doesn't mean the standard of living is going up

A recession is a significant decline in economic activity across the economy, typically lasting for a sustained period. It is caused by a decrease in the **gross domestic product** (GDP – the value of the goods and services the nation produces), employment, investment, and other economic indicators. During a recession, businesses may reduce production, consumers may cut back on spending, and overall economic growth slows down or contracts.

It is important to understand that not being in a recession doesn't automatically mean everybody's standard of living is kept at the same level or goes up. It just means the economy is doing well. Possibly just making the rich richer and the poor poorer.

The standard of living refers to the level of comfort, prosperity, and quality of life enjoyed by individuals, households, or society as a whole. It encompasses various factors such as income, access to education, healthcare, housing, and other essential goods and services. The standard of living is a subjective and multidimensional concept, considering not only material well-being but also personal satisfaction, social well-being, and overall life satisfaction. Assessing the standard of living involves considering a combination of these factors to understand the well-being and quality of life of individuals or a population. It is an essential metric for evaluating a society's overall prosperity and development.

Public services controlled by the public

I think critical infrastructure, including roads, railways, and healthcare systems ought to be in the ownership of the citizens. Public services, the military, institutions, and the economy should be structured and governed with the welfare of the citizens in mind. In a dictatorship and often in so called "wannabe democracies", these elements are manipulated to generate income for privileged groups. Even nature itself is reduced to a source of profit, with these groups selling water and engineering crops with built-in self-destruct mechanisms.

Government debt

Tax avoidance by privileged groups and poor financial management compel governments to seek loans from these very groups. They need them to sustain vital social services and healthcare. Public assets, like transportation infrastructure, are privatised and sold to privileged groups. Credit ratings indicate the probability that a country will pay its debts. In addition to purely economic data, they take into account political, social and even cultural factors. An oil-rich country cursed with a despotic government, endemic warfare and a corrupt judicial system will usually receive a low credit rating.

A cost of living crisis is an inequality crisis.

There was never a single moment in history where a small group of wealthy people got so much richer in a short period as they have in the last 15 years. When asset costs are high and ordinary people have no assets at all, they need to work. Many jobs are where privileged groups live, so living costs in these cities are high. Cities without rich people very often cease to work economically. When we can't pay for our assets anymore – privileged groups pick them up for "peanuts", at least for them. And rent them back to us at high rates. I think if ordinary people are not going to get involved in the economy now, they will lose all their assets and money. I think austerity is a government choice. I believe it is the decision of the government not to tax the privileged groups.

Interesting facts

Conservative estimate of money spent on **Covid-19:**

U.S. $2.6 trillion / $600 per citizen

U.K. $540 billion / $6, 750 per citizen

Germany $513 billion / $6160 per citizen

The total **cost of bank bailouts** during the financial crisis in 2008:

UK: over $168 billion.

US: The initial authorization for the "Troubled Asset Relief Program" in the US was up to $700 billion.

Germany: The bailout of German banks hit by the financial crisis cost German citizens at least $44bn.

Public liabilities

Public liabilities refer to the financial obligations and debts incurred by a government in the course of its operations. These liabilities encompass various forms of debt, including government bonds, loans, and other types of finance that represent the government's indebtedness to external entities or its citizens. Managing public liabilities is crucial for maintaining fiscal responsibility and sustainability in a government's financial operations. The actual costs of public liabilities are frequently concealed.

Environmental clean-up costs: The costs associated with cleaning up environmental pollution or hazards may not always be immediately visible or accurately accounted for.

Infrastructure maintenance: Concealed costs can arise when maintenance of public infrastructure, such as roads, bridges, and public buildings, is deferred or not adequately funded.

Public health crisis management: Costs related to managing and recovering from public health crises, like pandemics, may not always be fully disclosed upfront.

Pension liabilities: Future pension obligations for public employees may still need to be fully funded, leading to concealed liabilities that surface over time.

Contingent liabilities: These are potential liabilities that may or may not occur, such as legal claims against the government, and their costs can be uncertain and hidden.

Public-private partnerships (PPPs): Costs associated with PPPs may be somewhat transparent, leading to potential hidden liabilities for the public sector.

Subsidies and grants: The true costs of subsidies or grants may always only sometimes be apparent due to various accounting practices and reporting methods.

Long-term debt obligations: Future debt obligations may not be fully disclosed, leading to hidden costs that become apparent over time.

Natural disaster recovery: Costs associated with the recovery and rebuilding efforts after natural disasters may be estimated or underestimated initially.

Security and defence spending: Certain defence and security-related costs may need to be fully transparent, especially in classified or sensitive areas.

Ordinary citizens shoulder interest on government debt. This results in budget deficits – that is, government-level shortfalls of money – that eventually spiral out of control, leaving citizens to bear the burden.

Do you want an economy where only the privileged groups get richer? Or do you want an economy where everybody can get rich?

Interesting facts

The rate of home ownership in the UK has fallen from 73 percent since 2007. The time taken to save for a deposit for a house on an average wage:

in 1980: 3 years

in 2022: 24 years

2.4 Social capital

Religion and social capital

Social collectives such as religious communities can serve as reservoirs of social capital, contributing to the creation of public goods for the collective welfare.

What social groups produce

Social capital refers to the networks, relationships, and social bonds within a community or society that contribute to cooperation, trust, and shared values. It encompasses the social connections, norms, and mutual understanding that facilitate collective action and collaboration. High social capital is associated

with increased social cohesion, civic engagement, and the ability of a community to address common challenges effectively. This can improve the performance and the evolution of communities.

Abuse of social capital

Some citizens, including privileged groups, can exploit groups like religious communities to amass wealth and promote their personal interests. They take advantage of the tax and other benefits provided to these communities due to their capacity to generate social capital, diverting these advantages for their private benefit. Instances of charity misconduct for example include embezzlement, misappropriation of funds, or using charitable resources for personal expenses. Such cases can erode public trust and have led to increased scrutiny on the governance and transparency of charitable organisations. It's important to recognize that the majority of charities operate ethically and play a crucial role in society, but occasional misconduct can occur.

3. Recognising dictatorship

3.1 Legitimate politician or dictator?

We are all "superior"

We think we are superior to others, deserve more, should give less and are destined to rule everyone. But only sometimes. Mostly, we are humble, generous and respectful. Mindful of our dark desires, we try to put them aside.

Narcissistic personality disorder

There are individuals who consistently believe in their superiority, entitlement to more, aversion to giving, and a destiny to rule over others. "Narcissistic personality disorder" is a long-term personality disorder marked by damaging behaviour, including exaggerated self-importance, an insatiable need for admiration, and a lack of empathy. It's our responsibility to ensure that individuals with mental illnesses receive therapy rather than being placed in positions of power. The more narcissistic an individual is, the more damaging their impact on the community.

The cruel clown

Some politicians exploit our dark emotions and fantasies. The "cruel clown" politician acts as a cunning trickster, delivering carefully crafted, divisive messages, often tinged with racism and war rhetoric. They are usually orchestrated by the best PR agencies and funded by tax-avoiding billionaire-privileged groups. Privileged groups use them to divert attention from potential alternatives to their policies. The cruel clown appears as though they operate with impunity, engaging in behaviours like bullying, embezzlement, and manipulation. They are sometimes hailed as a heroic figure by frustrated, irate citizens. The cruel clown claims to be on the side of "the people" but doesn't accept the rights or opinions of anyone who doesn't support them.

Interesting quote

"It makes no difference whatsoever: whether they laugh at us or revile us ... whether they represent us as clowns or criminals; the main thing is that they mention us, that they concern themselves with us again and again ..."

Hitler

Political dictators

Dictators come to power in military juntas, one-party states, or dominant-party states. They often use the proclamation of a state of emergency to rule by decree. Dictators hold and abuse an extraordinary amount of personal power. They can have left—, right-wing, or a-political views. They often foster a cult of personality.

Corporate dictators

Corporate dictators rise to power on the back of money and data. The bigger a company is, the more data and computing power it gets, the more efficient it becomes. They are self-appointed, with no governing body checking their activities. They keep their power by controlling the mass media, even influencing elections. This influence is often through financial contributions, lobbying, or support for political candidates or causes. One notable example is the influence of corporations through political action committees (PACs) or donations to campaigns, which can impact the political landscape. Corporations often impact civil liberties; they repress political opponents and do not abide by the rule of law. They spy on citizens as well as restricting or completely removing our personal freedoms. They often foster a cult of personality.

Privileged groups: easy to identify

Who wields control over information, natural resources, and food? Who holds the reins of financial power? Do their relatives occupy seats in the parliament? A list of the connections of the most influential individuals and their associations conveys more about the corruption of a state than conducting ten surveys on corruption.

3.2 Corporate power

Corporation or Mafia?

The actions of privileged groups range from completely legitimate businesses to creating concentration camps and worse. Very often, they create organisations with totalitarian structures that have no responsibility to anyone, no transparency and no morals. They keep these organisations hidden from others.

Corporations: more powerful than governments

Concentrated power can take many forms and is always a threat to democracy. Corporations accumulate political power and wealth. They make more money and are more powerful than countries today. But unlike governments they are not elected by citizens. What if the economy of the future solely depends on capital and intellectual ownership executed by machines? A centrally planned, state-controlled economy where machines do the work? Is this better than complicated, rights-obsessed democracies?

A **monopoly** refers to a situation in which a single company or entity has exclusive control over the supply of a particular product or service in a market. In other words, it's when one company dominates an entire industry without facing significant competition.

Key characteristics of a monopoly include:

Single Seller: There is only one seller or provider of a product or service in the market, giving them significant market power.

No Close Substitutes: Consumers have limited or no alternative options to choose from, as there are no close substitutes available for the monopolised product or service.

Price Control: The monopolist has the ability to set prices independently, typically leading to higher prices for consumers compared to competitive markets.

Barriers to Entry: Entry into the market by potential competitors is difficult due to factors such as high startup costs, exclusive access to resources, or legal barriers.

Monopolies can arise naturally due to factors such as technological innovation or economies of scale, but they can also result from anti-competitive behaviour or government regulation. While monopolies may increase profits for the monopolist, they can also result in reduced consumer choice, higher prices, and decreased innovation. Therefore, governments often regulate or break up monopolies to promote competition and protect consumer interests.

Corporations are the people's masters

Today's government is mostly a government of corporations, by corporations and for corporations. The "corporation government" undermines the justice and integrity of democracy. Ithink it is a dictatorship of self-glorification and capital for privileged groups. The people making the decisions aren't those who have to live with the consequences.

The offshore dictatorship

By creating complex systems of income and inheritance tax avoidance, privileged groups cement their power. Billionaire tax avoiders often acquired their capital through inherited wealth, exclusive control of crucial assets or service monopolies, unbundling and commercialising public assets. Their power exists in the secretive, extraterritorial legal

space of offshore companies and accounts, beyond the control of any country. This financial, hypermobile capital rules the new global state.

Missing money

The biggest injustice of tax avoidance is how it creates inequality and de-funds public services.In poorer countries where wages – and accordingly individual income taxes – are low, governments depend much more heavily on corporation tax. Many of these countries have a vast wealth in natural resources. Tax havens allow companies to plunder these resources whilst paying very little to the country in return. We miss out on billions in spending for roads, schools, the health system and much else. Privileged groups stand in the way of policies that would improve life for people in general. I think if we do not redistribute the wealth the inequality, living standards, and experiential values will not improve. Governments can only regulate tax laws within their own borders, while companies often take advantage of more lenient tax regulations in other countries. Consequently, tax avoidance is a problem affecting both corporations and consumers. By showing a commitment to paying fair taxes, companies enable countries to impose equitable rates and contribute to the national infrastructure and resources from which they benefit

Interesting facts

The world loses the equivalent of a nurse's annual salary to a tax haven every second, and will lose nearly $5 trillion in the next 10 years, according to the Tax Justice Network.

In 2021, up to half a billion pounds could have been lost to the UK exchequer from the corporation tax avoidance of just one company, Amazon. The U.K. government estimates that in 2019-20, the financial loss from tax avoidance was £1.5 billion

Leading economists agree that there is no economic justification for tax havens. In 2016, over 300 economists (organised by Oxfam) wrote to the world's leaders saying that havens "served no useful economic purpose" and "are distorting the working of the global economy."

Countries classed as tax havens

Algeria, American Samoa, Angola, Anguilla, Antigua and Barbuda, Aruba, Bahamas, Bangladesh, Barbados, Belarus, Belize, Bermuda, Bolivia, British Virgin Islands, Brunei, Cameroon, Cayman Islands, Cook Islands, Costa Rica, Curacao, Cyprus, Estonia, Fiji, Gambia, Gibraltar, Guam, Guatemala, Guernsey, Hong Kong, Hungary, Ireland, Isle of Man, Jersey, Jordan, Kuwait, Latvia, Lebanon, Liberia, Liechtenstein, Luxembourg, Maldives, Malta, Marshall Islands, Mauritius, Monaco, Montenegro, Montserrat, Namibia, Netherlands, Oman, Palau, Panama, Puerto Rico, Qatar, Russia, Rwanda, Samoa, Seychelles, Singapore, Sri Lanka, St Lucia, St. Kitts and Nevis, Switzerland, Thailand, Trinidad and Tobago, Turks and Caicos Islands, UAE, US Virgin Islands, Vanuatu, Venezuela, Vietnam

Source: Ethical Consumer

Illegal income

A form of extreme authoritarian capitalism is spreading its influence in countries across the globe. Even organised crime can operate unhindered, as long as their actions do not pose a threat to privileged groups. Collaborating closely with such criminal organisations grants these privileged groups access to a range of specialists, including snipers, explosives  experts, computer hackers, contract killers, human traffickers, money launderers, and drug networks. Collaborative criminal activities with these gangs generate revenue for the privileged groups.

Organised crime refers to criminal activities that are planned, coordinated, and carried out by groups or networks of individuals for financial gain or power. These groups often operate through hierarchical structures and engage in various illegal activities such as drug trafficking, human trafficking, money laundering, extortion, racketeering, and cybercrime.

Key characteristics of organised crime include:

Structured Organisation: Criminal groups have well-defined roles and hierarchies, with leaders, enforcers, and members responsible for different aspects of their operations.

Continuity and Persistence: Organised crime groups engage in illegal activities over an extended period, often adapting their strategies to evade law enforcement and maintain their profitability.

Global Reach: Many organised crime syndicates operate internationally, taking advantage of globalisation to expand their illicit activities across borders.

Violence and Intimidation: Violence, threats, and intimidation are common tactics used by organised crime groups to control territories, eliminate rivals, and coerce victims.

Corruption and Infiltration: Organised crime often seeks to corrupt public officials, law enforcement, and businesses to facilitate their operations and evade detection.

Combating organised crime requires cooperation and co-ordination among law enforcement agencies, governments, and international organisations to disrupt criminal networks, prosecute offenders, and address the underlying factors that enable their activities.

What do you think?

Do you think your government has links to organised crime?

Do you think your local takeaway is paying "protection money" or something similar?

3.3 Corruption

Political and economic corruption

It's a big challenge to democracy when basic public goods are only distributed to privileged groups instead of to all citizens. When corruption becomes the norm in a society, its democratic nature diminishes.

Cronyism

Cronyism refers to the practice of favouring close friends, associates, or relatives, especially in politics or business, often to the detriment of merit-based decision-making. In the context of democracy, cronyism is considered a form of corruption, as it involves the misuse of power and resources for personal or close-knit network gains rather than serving the broader public interest. In a healthy democracy,

transparency, accountability, and the rule of law are essential safeguards against cronyism. Key characteristics of cronyism in a democratic setting include:

Nepotism and favouritism: Cronyism involves the unfair granting of favours, opportunities, or privileges to individuals based on personal relationships rather than on their qualifications, skills, or merit.

Abuse of power: Those in positions of power, whether in government or other influential sectors, may engage in cronyism by using their authority to benefit friends or associates, giving them preferential treatment in terms of contracts, appointments, or other benefits.

Undermining achievement: In a democratic system that values an achievement-based system, cronyism undermines the principles of fair competition and the selection of individuals based on their abilities, qualifications, and achievements.

Negative impact on institutions: Cronyism can erode public trust in democratic institutions by creating a perception that by personal connections, which influence decision-making more than the public good. This can lead to a decline in the effectiveness and legitimacy of democratic processes.

Distortion of economic competition: In the business sector, cronyism can distort market competition by favouring certain companies or individuals through government contracts, subsidies, or regulatory advantages, irrespective of their competitiveness.

Corruption risks: Cronyism is often associated with corruption, as it involves the potential misuse of public resources or positions for personal gain. This can lead to a lack of accountability and transparency in decision-making processes.

Lobbying

Most citizens don't get to spend time with their representatives. The professional lobbyists for big corporations do. They have the resources to pamper politicians and influence them. I think the line between lobbying and corruption is very, very thin.

Interesting fact

Some politicians in the UK are approached by lobbyists 100 times per week. Google spent over $16 million lobbying the US government in 2015.

Abuse of the army

I think the military should be structured and overseen to ensure the welfare of citizens. The primary goal is safeguarding them and providing aid in humanitarian and environmental crises. Unfortunately, significant sums are unjustifiably channelled to arms manufacturers owned by privileged groups. These also exploit the military to steal resources from other nations

under the guise of defending human rights. In this process, millions of lives are lost, and environmental catastrophes emerge. Subsequently, substantial funds are allocated to privileged groups' corporations to rebuild the nations they have devastated. I think all of these actions should be regarded as war crimes, and those responsible should be held accountable.

Corporations now run off-the-shelf armies to safeguard their interests. Capital trickles away from dictatorial states that fail to defend private individuals and their property. Instead, it flows into states upholding the rule of law and private property.

Interesting fact

The British state did not conquer the Indian subcontinent; rather, it was the mercenary army of the British East India Company that achieved this. The company maintained a massive military force of up to 350, 000 soldiers, significantly outnumbering the armed forces of the British monarchy.

Interesting quote

"democratic armies fight better than armies aristocratically organised and autocratically governed' and that 'the armies of nations in which the mass of the people determine legislation, elect their public servants, and settle questions of peace and war, fight better than the armies of an autocrat who rules by right of birth and by commission from the Almighty.' "

Charles W. Eliot
(president of Harvard from 1869 to 1909)

What do you think?

Has your country been involved in a war recently, and why?

4. Privileged groups and the danger they pose for democracy

4.1 Privileged groups: who are they?
What is a privileged group?

A privileged group is a small group of people who have power and access to resources that are not available to others. Their privileges may be based on factors such as race, gender, or social class. Examples of privileged groups include castes, orders, royals, self-appointed political leaders, and oligarchs. This does not mean people like doctors or high earners in a medium-sized company.

2000 people own the world

In Russia, oligarchs amassed their fortunes during the period of Russian privatisation in the 1990s. Over 90% of Chinese billionaires are affiliated with the Chinese Communist Party due to China's market-oriented reforms in the 1980s. In the United States, the wealthy often inherit wealth derived from endeavours in the railroads, oil, land, and the labour of enslaved individuals by their ancestors. In Arab nations, the 0.001% elite class derives billions from the oil industry, often representing the state. Affluent Europeans typically fall into categories of company founders, individuals from the financial sector, or those who inherited wealth from forebears who acquired it by exploiting colonies.

Self-perpetuating growth of surplus

Privileged groups ensure they receive more public resources than the average citizen. They gain more economic, political, and cultural power, which they can use to acquire an even larger share of resources. The percentage of income privileged groups need to spend on living is much lower. They save most of the money. A lot of poorer people – the rest of us, in comparison – need to work. When individuals belonging to privileged groups have bad intentions, they pose an even ,more significant threat to a democratic society.

We all think like privileged groups. Our affluence is often based on someone else's deprivation. We usually take our privileges for granted, and we should be more aware of how our lives are more accessible than those of others. We all support privileged groups by buying their products, working for them, and not checking if they pay taxes. We vote for politicians employed by them.

4.2 Staying in power, getting more pow-erful

Everything is helping privileged groups

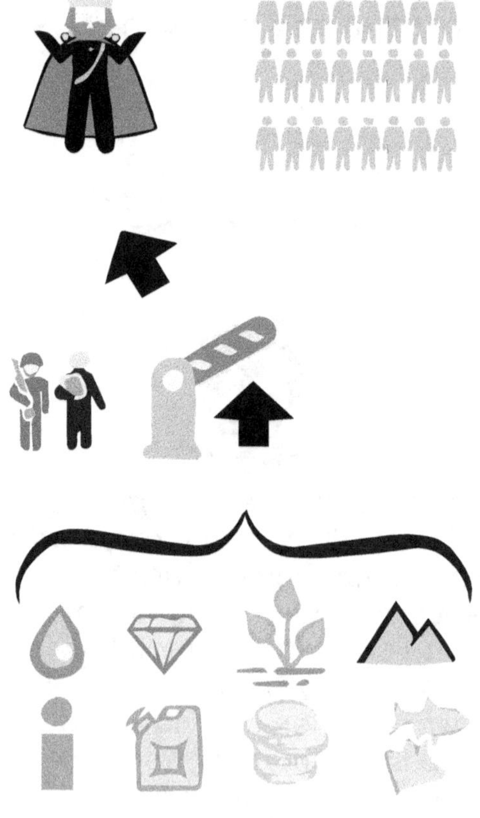

It's well documented that privileged groups ensure close co-operation between the educational system, the armed forces, landowners, and the clergy. This ensures that the privileged groups' control over the generation and distribution of public goods to them doesn't cease.

Trickle-down is a trick.

"Trickle-down economics" is an economic theory that suggests policies benefiting the wealthy and businesses will ultimately benefit the broader population. By reducing taxes on high-income individuals and corporations, these groups will have more resources to invest, create jobs, and stimulate economic growth. The resulting prosperity is expected to "trickle down" to lower-income individuals through increased employment opportunities and economic expansion. I think it's fair to say that the benefits of reduced taxes for privileged groups outweigh the benefits for all other citizens. Privileged groups have the resources and global strategy to avoid taxation, contributing nothing to society. Monopoly power and other preferential tax treatment also undermine the economy's efficiency. These preferential treatments for privileged groups can include lower tax rates, deductions, credits, or loopholes. This goes on to create new distortions, undermining efficiency and inequality even further.

Give citizens just enough privilege to keep them quiet

Privileged groups create limited ways for citizens to move up the status ladder. This is only to keep them striving to belong to the privileged group rather than using their energy to end the unequal treatment.

The illusion of democracy

Imagine: every four years a privileged group hand picks their favourite candidates to be voted as political leaders. Sophisticated psychological warfare techniques are applied to manufacture consent in the public and unwanted opinions are suppressed. Alternative candidates are intimidated, killed or simply deprived of resources. The energy of change is redirected and we are given the illusion of being in control. Or the privileged groups just make sure that everybody is too apathetic to vote.

1% charities

"With great power comes great responsibility" (according to Spider-Man's Uncle Ben). Some privileged groups become aware of the impact their corporations have on the world. But does their charity work really outweigh the ongoing damage they do to society and the environment?

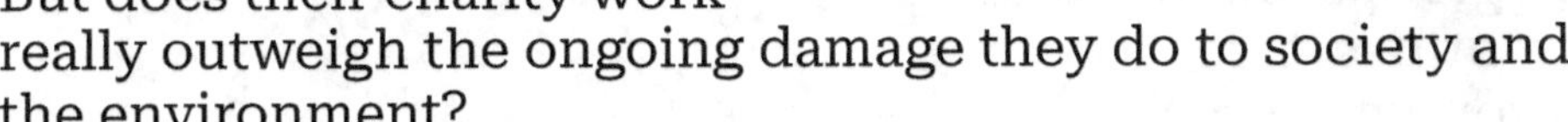

4.3 Causing the end of civilised life on Earth

Ruining the planet

The greatest danger for the planet is that most of the 2000 billionaires and their corporations not only ignore and contribute most to global boiling but actively fund campaigns to play down its disastrous consequences. We may contribute ourselves but this is nothing compared to the damage privileged groups with their corporations and luxury lifestyle cause.

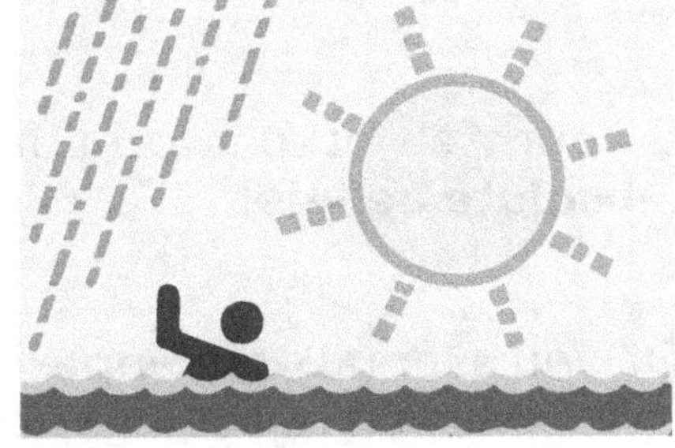

Privileged groups controlling wise elite democracy

In the "wise elite" model we met earlier, which most democracies are using, decision-making is delegated to a group selected by the citizens. In reality though, this group is selected by privileged groups and not citizens using bribes, threats and disinformation.

4.4 Using extremism to stay in power

What defines an extremist?

Consider the following questions, and the mindsets they represent:

Is your view of the world the only valid one? **(absolute beliefs)**

Do you ever talk to people you don't like, or do you see them as threats and reject any viewpoint they have? (demonisation of others)

Do you feel superior to others? **(us vs. them mentality)**

Do you subtly encourage violence and think it is justified? **(violence or advocacy of violence)**

Do you think that only certain groups cause all the evil in the world? **(conspiracy theories)**

Do you spend a lot of time online talking to like-minded people? **(isolation or radicalisation online)**

Do you think democracy should be abandoned so your goals can be achieved? **(rejection of democratic processes)**

Have you stopped spending time with friends and family because they don't share your beliefs? **(social withdrawal or alienation)**

Have you recently changed your appearance? **(sudden changes in behaviour or appearance)**

Are you a big fan of certain iconography (collections of signs and symbols)? (symbolism and iconography)

Then you are an extremist!

Disclaimer: It's important to note that displaying one or more of these signs does not necessarily mean someone is an extremist, as context and individual circumstances matter. However, recognising these indicators can help identify individuals who may be at risk of radicalisation and intervene before they become involved in harmful activities.

A breeding ground for extremism

The privileges of elite groups come at a cost for us: wage stagnation, loss of jobs and poor public services. As a result, we often end up having low self-esteem, feeling unfairly treated and humiliated. In addition to this, low birth rates (in rich countries), global mobility and impersonal inner city life break up families, familiar worlds and shared identities. Today, more than ever, we are craving for belonging. Hard times make people literally go insane, a fertile ground for extremism: a dictator arises, blaming problems on others and making false promises of rectifying "a rigged system".

Using extremism to stay in power

The main intention of privileged groups is to remain in power. They take advantage of fascist and nationalist tendencies in the population to do so. The wealth created through dodgy trusts in tax havens is used to support political marionettes and dictators, like the cruel clown characters, who often trade in far-right populism. Fascism rigs elections, typically comes to power with around 40 per cent support and uses control and intimidation to gain even more power. Very often they use democratic rights to come to power and dismantle them as soon they are in power.

Extremism does not do subtle.

Extremist leadership systems present themselves as the single source of truth. "We know who we are. And we know if you are one of us." Extremism suppresses debate within its ranks: "You are with us or against us!" There is nothing else:

no tolerance of minority positions but repression of internal complexity complemented by hatred for "external" others.

Conspiracy theories and extreme views

It is a human tendency to perceive unseen forces at work. A conspiracy theory is a proposed secret plot, usually by a powerful group of people with a sinister goal and only their interests. The explanation is always vague, and the plot is often large and important, of great political or social significance.

Weak wisdom

When we find it difficult to judge when to trust and when to be sceptical, when to differentiate between credible and non-credible sources, we will get into trouble. It gets even worse if we immediately disregard sources that might contradict our views. We live in a dangerous fantasy if our ability for deep critical thinking is missing. And we are not prepared to change our minds when our experiments fail. If no amount of evidence is ever enough to make us change our minds that we "know" the Earth is flat, for example.

Trauma, belonging and the need to be happy.

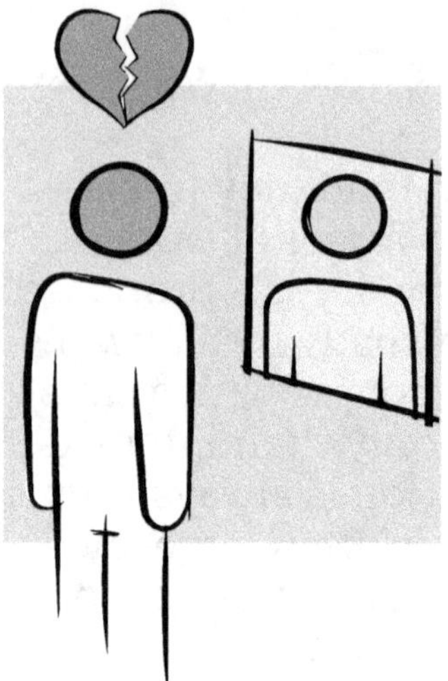

Big lies work only in lonely minds. A mind with a sense of universal responsibility is the exact opposite. Extremism is born out of insecurity and the feeling of being left out: we all want to feel safe, secure and autonomous in the world that we live in. We have a need for knowledge and certainty of information. We want to feel good about ourselves and the group we belong to. Sometimes to the extreme that we want to feel superior to others.

The extremist mindset is marked by the following:

-   unrealistic self-esteem and narcissism

-   feeling of intellectual superiority

-   overinflated sense of the importance of the group we belong to, but at the same time, the feeling that this group is under appreciated.

84

From a feeling of unrealistic superiority to dehumanising others

Having those sorts of beliefs, we can maintain the idea that our group is good, moral and upstanding whereas others are not. In contrast, others are the evildoers ruining it for everybody else. This is the first step in dehumanising "the other" and justifying acts of violence, suppression dehumanising "the other" and justifying acts of violence, suppression, or worse.

Gradually given the taste for savagery.

When citizens stop feeling like they are part of the community, not being heard, and seeing problems as complex and remain unresolved, they can have a "romantic" longing for somebody who will solve all their problems: the "strong ruler." Fascism uses this longing to enhance citizens' fear, suggesting simple solutions - until they get a seat in the parliament.

In a good democracy, fascism doesn't happen overnight. It creeps in very slowly, habituating us to atrocities normally not allowed to happen. From racist language to violence against minorities to concentration camps. Atrocities are more accessible to justify if they are committed against an "inferior race." This sort of extermination of people is often claimed to be justified by the purpose of progress and enlightenment.

Fascist checklist

-powerful, robust nationalism

-disdain for human rights -vilification of enemies as a unifying cause

-supremacy of the military

-rampant sexism

-controlled mass media

-obsession with national security -religion and government intertwined

-corporate power protected, labour power suppressed

-disdain for intellectuals and the arts

-obsession with crime and punishment

-rampant crony-ism and corruption.

5. Control techniques

5.1 Using surveillance technology

Surveillance capitalism

Tools like facial and bionic recognition systems, GPS data, voice recordings, web browser history, behavioural data and credit ratings are combined and analysed in order to make money from us. This data predicts products we might buy, potential future behaviour and future illnesses.

Designing the perfect police state

Using the infrastructure created by surveillance capitalism, the perfect police state is first introduced to "protect us" from terrorists – then criminals, activists, and finally any opposition, like people not voting for the "right" party. The internet acts as a real-time, privately run digital intelligence service. Sophisticated surveillance infrastructure, like facial recognition, location data, satellite tracking,, personal, and personal data, are combined with AI. Mobiles are used as real-time people-tracking devices. Software predicts behaviour and AI triggers the appropriate reaction to prevent it before it occurs. Anything is believable and unknowable simultaneously as no independent information and discussion exist.

5.2 Creating apathy

Apathy is the greatest, most significant threat to democracy.

The population's lack of interest and participation is the biggest challenge for any democracy. Change is unlikely when most people are satisfied with how things are. If we don't feel personally affected and don't care about others, nothing will improve. A democracy can't thrive without active participation and commitment from the people. Patriotism is more

than waving a flag. It's proactively working to make society more democratic, more just, less racist, and more humane. Promote a more humane society that always speaks out about social injustice. Unfortunately, we often willingly let others handle our responsibilities. We have to evolve from watching football to playing the match ourselves, based on everyone's level of competence.

Distraction and consumerism

A cheap alternative is to ensure no one cares who is in control: privileged groups promote escapism, into media, for example, as long as they are not educational or thought-provoking. They advertise the consumption of products for the sake of distraction. Privileged groups make sure the truth is drowned in a sea of pleasure and fear, an information overload, tempting us to just "switch off." This ends in the privileged group's favourite result: apathy.

Creating apathy using information overload

Privileged groups make sure the truth is drowned in a sea of irrelevance. Reading long texts about complex ideas or concepts is discouraged. Information critical of privileged groups or proves a threat to their power is banned.

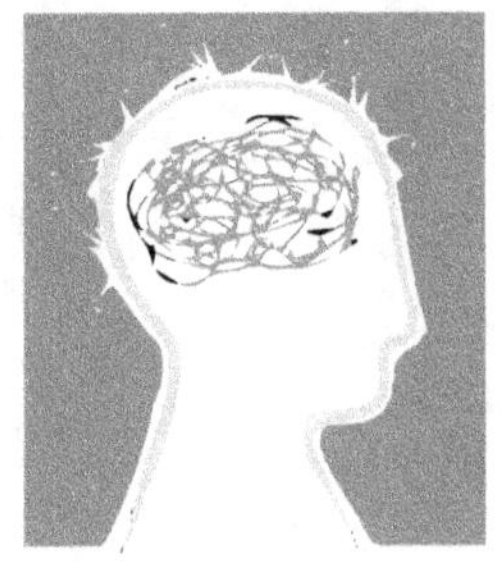

Interesting fact

The turnout of eligible voters in the UK population:

1950: 83.9%

2001: 59.4%

2015: 66.2 %

2017: 68.7 %

5.3 Psychological control

Simple indoctrination

Democracy has transformed due to the evolving technology of information dissemination. Open discourse has been supplanted by a form of psychological warfare, where daily lies are disseminated through news and media channels. Personalised psychometric messaging tactics are employed to distract, misinform, and indoctrinate the public, often using social media bots.

The extremists' scheme: psychometric messaging tactics

Extremism needs a propaganda machine (social media are ideal for this) to create a secret world of "alternative facts" for its followers. It divides citizens into groups of extreme and exclusive tribes. It builds and builds up a sense of false threat from another group, dehumanising the members of that group.

They are deliberately causing emotional upset to stop analytical thinking.

This method involves deliberately cultivating outrage, fear, and suspicion among specific ethnic and religious groups by meticulously targeting these demographics with divisive narratives. Social media and news outlets contribute to the creation of individualised "echo chambers," exposing us only to information that aligns with our existing beliefs.

Divide and conquer—isolate

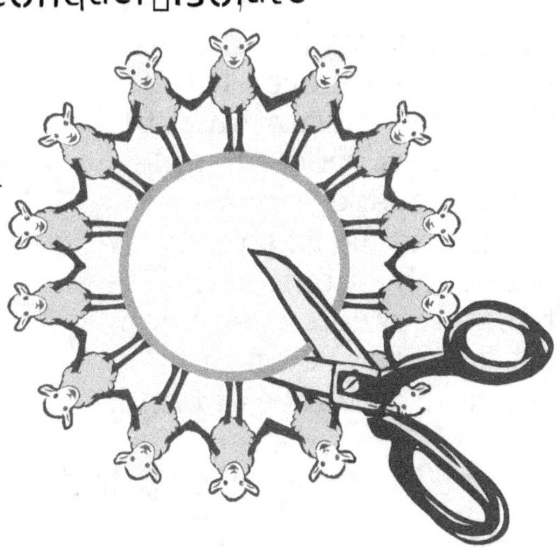

Activities that might threaten existing power structures, like independent thinking and discussion, are discouraged. Everything is done to divide communities and networks, posing a threat. Critical individuals are isolated.

Fear and intimidation

The prospect of worsening our own situation will block any thought of criticism right at the start. The fear of prison maintains the social order while creating another source of income for privileged groups: critics are silenced with the threat of publishing embarrassing personal details. We fear for our children's future; this fear makes us accept low wages and social instability.

Forcing the unthinkable

Privileged groups indoctrinate us to not even think about certain "unthinkable" subjects. A good example is how most citizens accept our particularist society. We can reach a point of indoctrination where even facts can't start a thought process and a change of mind.

Deep indoctrination

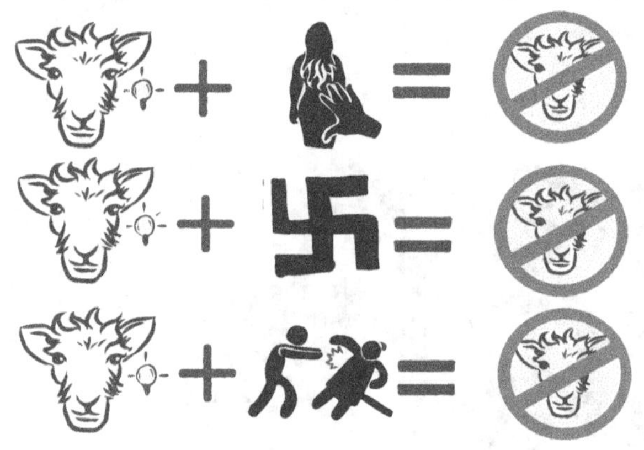

A critical person/group or concept is paired by the privileged groups with a lie – the lie relating a non-acceptable concept—rape, adultery, drug abuse, fascism, for example. As a result, we won't even listen to what a critical person/group has to say.

Promoting of words

Words define our thoughts, carrying a set of assumptions, connotations, and preconceptions. They have a history attached. Take, for example, the words expat/immigrant or freedom fighter/terrorist. Privileged groups promote the use of certain words to divide and indoctrinate us. Language allows us to persuade others that appearances are a reality.

Decision habits

"Decision habits" are being used by privileged groups to manipulate us. We tend to believe things because many others believe them, ignore general information, and focus on information only relating to a certain particular situation. We do not revise our opinions sufficiently when presented with new evidence and draw different conclusions from the same information depending on how that information is presented.

Conscience-distorting experts

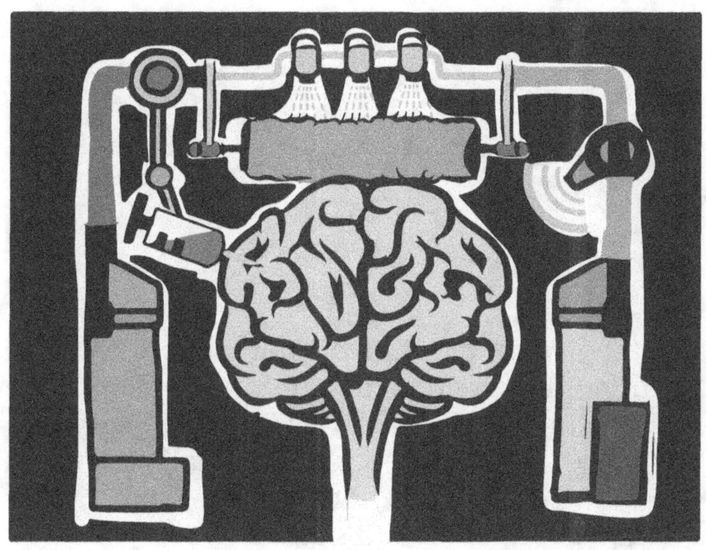

Propaganda presented to us is researched by top scientists, tailored based on our psychological profiles and designed by highly skilled advertising specialists. Little surprise, we don't even notice it.

We get frustrated with the environment the privileged groups create. To diffuse this anger, they encourage hate "energy" onto a target that is never them, based on race, nationality, political party etc). This target is periodically swapped and the real reason for the poor environment – the actions of those privileged groups – is concealed.

5.4 10 strategies of mind manipulation

Sylvain Timsit's "10 Strategies of Mind Manipulation" list appeared on his website, Syti.net, in 2002. It highlights the various methods used to manipulate public opinion and maintain control over the population.

1. The strategy of distraction

Control is achieved by diverting our minds from major problems through continuous bombardment with distractions and insignificant information. This keeps our minds busy, draws away from reality with no time to think, and prevents us from learning anything of real importance.

2. Creating problems and then offering the solutions

"Terrorists will take your liberties, that's why you have to renounce them to the surveillance state!" Creating a "problem" is planned to cause a specific reaction from us, with the aim that this is the source of the measures we want to accept. For example, letting urban violence intensify and pay for organised attacks, with the aim of the public backing new security laws, including the detriment of freedom. Or to create an economic crisis to demolish and dismantle social and public services so that the public will accept it as a necessary evil. The evil clowns employed by privileged groups will much more likely take our liberties than terrorists.

3. The strategy of graduation

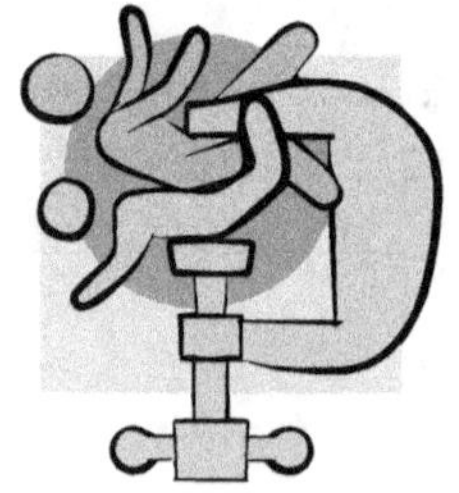

Applying unacceptable measures gradually, over consecutive years, to make us accept them: wages that no longer guarantee dignified incomes, corporations not paying any taxes, no public services, no health insurance.

4. The strategy of deferral

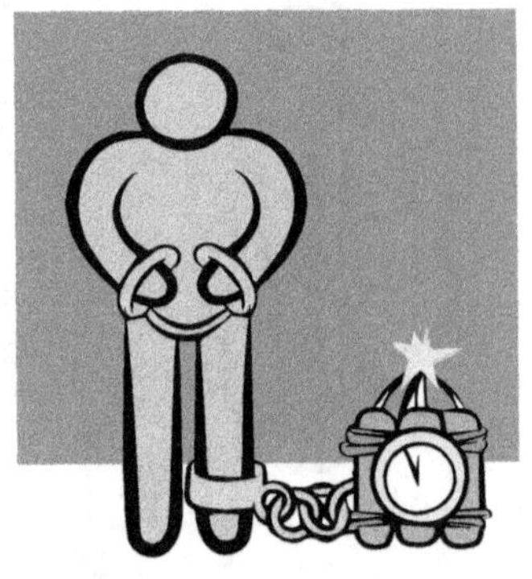

Get an unpopular decision accepted by presenting it as "painful and necessary", gaining public acceptance, in the moment, for future application. In essence, the strategy of deferral allows politicians to navigate complex and controversial issues by delaying action, often in the hopes that future circumstances will be more favourable for decision-making. However, deferral can also lead to inertia, exacerbate problems, and erode public trust if perceived as avoiding responsibility or failing to address urgent challenges.

Interesting to know:

The strategy of deferral is a common tactic in politics worldwide. Here are a few examples:

Budgetary Issues: Politicians may defer making tough decisions on budgetary matters, such as raising taxes or cutting spending, by passing temporary measures or postponing decisions to future sessions.

Healthcare Reform: Governments may delay implementing comprehensive healthcare reform due to its complexity and potential political backlash, opting instead for incremental changes or deferring action to future administrations.

Infrastructure Investment: Decision-makers might defer investing in critical infrastructure projects, such as roads or bridges, due to budget constraints or disagreements over funding sources, leading to delays in much-needed improvements.

Climate Change Policy: Some governments may defer implementing ambitious climate change policies, such as carbon pricing or emissions reduction targets, due to concerns about economic impact or resistance from industries.

Electoral Reforms: Politicians may postpone addressing electoral reforms, such as campaign finance regulations or voting rights, in favour of maintaining the status quo or deferring action to independent commissions or study groups.

Foreign Policy Decisions: Governments may defer taking decisive action on foreign policy issues, such as military interventions or diplomatic negotiations, due to uncertainties about international alliances, domestic support, or the potential consequences of intervention.

Social Issues: Policymakers may defer addressing contentious social issues, such as immigration reform or LGBTQ+ rights, to avoid polarising debates or risking political backlash from certain constituencies.

5. Treat the public like children

Using speeches, arguments, characters and a particularly childish intonation, many times suggesting weakness, as if citizens are under 12 years old. Then we then tend to respond or react without a critical sense, as if we are actually under 12.

6. Using emotional aspect much more than reflection

Using emotions to provoke a short circuit on rational analysis and finally the critical sense of the individual. Additionally, the use of emotional register allows the unconscious access door to implant or inject ideas, desires, fears and fears, compulsions, or induce behaviours.

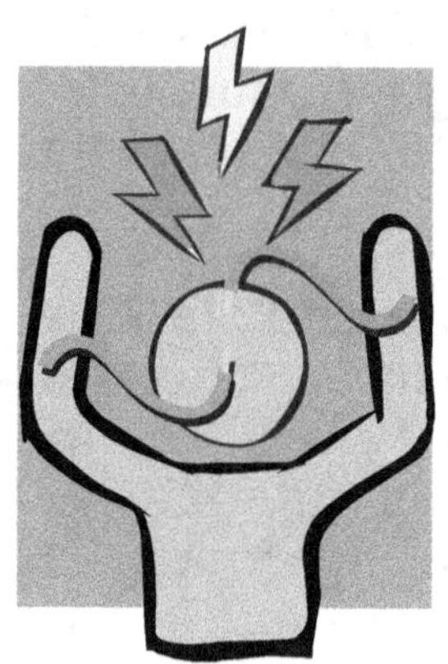

7. Keeping the public in uneducated ignorance

Making us incapable of understanding the technologies and methods used to control and enslave us. The quality of education given to us is deliberately designed to be as poor and mediocre as possible: So that meaningful, good education does not enable us to seriously question existing power structures.

8. Stimulating the public to be complacent with mediocrity

Pushing us to think it's fashionable to be stupid, vulgar and ignorant.

9. Strengthening self-guilt

Making the individual believe that they are the cause of their own disgrace, because of insufficient intelligence, skills or efforts. So, instead of questioning existing power structures, individuals devalue and blame themselves, which in turn creates a depressive state, one of whose effects is to inhibit them from taking action. Without action there is no change!

10. Knowing us better than we know ourselves

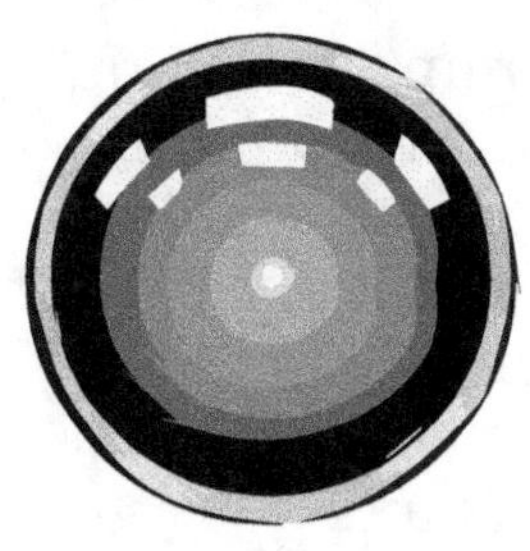

There is a growing gap between public knowledge and the knowledge possessed and used by the privileged groups. Thanks to biology, neurobiology, and applied psychology, they have enjoyed advanced knowledge of the human being, both in its physical and psychological form. The system has managed to learn more about us than we know about ourselves. This means that, in most cases, the system exercises greater control and greater power over individuals, greater than that which the same individuals exercise over themselves.

What do you think?

How is it that we have so much information, but know so little?

5.5 Using violence

Controlled behaviour using terror

A "social credit" system is implemented to rate the trustworthiness of its citizens: credit rating, adherence to the law, "social sincerity". If you haven't complied you get blacklisted. The lists are shared publicly and you are blocked from borrowing money, booking flights, accessing healthcare and voting. Blacklisted enterprises are excluded from government contracts or business credits. Billboards and social media advertise role models. This forges an environment where keeping the privileged groups happy is glorified. And we will – because everyone is terrified.

Using violence to control citizens

Physical violence, imprisonment, social and economical strangling, torture, surveillance... all of it is used by privileged groups. After all, their main intention is to remain in power. Often, the legal system leaves them unpunished.

The few who inform themselves and voice anything critical of privileged groups are intimidated, imprisoned or worse. We like to decide for ourselves. To be violently forced to do something or seeing others being forced results in opposition. Suppressing citizens with violence often gets too expensive for privileged groups. That's why they also use other, cheaper techniques.

5.6 Stories help privileged groups stay in power

Ideologies are stories

An ideology is a story producing emotions and a happy ending. It is fiction – not reality. It tries to make people act. Its function is to help us make sense of the world – and as history and the world moves on, it is very often proved false. Stories can captivate, spark emotions, motivate even give a deep desire to change. They can change the way we see the world – in both positive and negative ways.

Ideology, opinion formation and management

Facts are not what move most people to change – stories are. Privileged groups promote stories that will push public opinion in their desired direction. They claim that they have the monopoly of rationality and realism – everything else is utopianism, unreasonable, regression, stupidity. The virtues of debate and conflicting perspectives are discredited.

Economic models are stories

We are people not machines: most current economic models are based on idealised, reduced versions of a complex human reality. They are stories, trying to motivate us to invest in something or not, not based on reality.Stories are a universal way of communicating and connecting with each other on a deep emotional level.

5.7 Extremist stories

Extremists stories have implausible endings

"Follow an omnipresent and omnipotent leader, whose single-handed guidance helps the nation to thrive and be happy." Or: "Let's return to an idealised version of the past and build a wall." Or: "It will be a never-ending story of national strength, happiness and economic stability if you vote for this political party." Unfortunately millions actually do believe these exact stories.

Ideology: "Social Darwinism"

The notion of *"survival of the fittest [the privileged groups], therefore you are all nature's failed experiments!"* represents a distortion of Charles Darwin's theories, notably employed by the Nazis to rationalise concentration camps. In the natural world, mutual reliance and cooperation are the norm, with survival of social species determined by collective, altruistic, and emotionally intelligent groups rather than sheer strength. Human compassion naturally emerges following disasters like tsunamis or hurricanes. In society, an added layer comes into play where institutions foster cooperation among individuals.

Extremists focus on culture

Culture rather than economics is at the centre of today's extremist ideology:

"Your culture and social environment is under threat from X. There is no other option, you must use violence to defend it. Once X is eliminated, you can live happily ever after." Just another implausible story with a horrible ending.

6. New foundations for a democracy

6.1 Be the change you want to see: we must start with ourselves

Inner evolution is revolution: cultivate sanity and intelligence

Even with the noblest of intentions, circumstances can still take a disastrous turn. Similar to advertising, the psychological warfare employed by privileged groups is strategically crafted to manipulate our most profound fears, insecurities, and hidden desires, often stoking anger and fostering division. It takes a lot of work to withdraw from this pull and form our own opinions, working on our minds, constantly checking that fiction does not replace truth. To enact lasting change, we must progress from impulsive, unprocessed emotions to becoming well informed, composed, compassionate, and collectively minded decision-makers. It is only when a substantial majority of us adheres to these higher ethical standards that long-term transformation can occur.

Put the money where our mouth is!

The fight is not necessarily with privileged groups. The fight is with ourselves. Stop thinking of our own gain and nothing else: we can choose better banks, produce environmentally friendly energy instead of buying it from privileged groups, and eat a vegetarian diet. Our approach must be to examine, train and cure our own minds first. And give our money only to companies with good ethical values and a concern for our planet. Flying long haul ten times a year and then going to an Extinction Rebellion event feels like a joke to me.

6.2 Triggering change in social interaction with others

We often meet people who think their behaviour is perfectly ok. (And others meet us and our behaviour.) People with no consideration for us that even deny our very existence. I think the only way for us to deal with them and for them to deal with us is to remember an ideal of humanity while empathetically acknowledging the reality. We are not going to change the other (at least not in that moment) but we have the power to make the best out of any situation. Even if the outcome is still very bleak. At least we can have no regrets, having tried our best and leave it to the subtleties of the complex karmic network of cause and conditions to produce the inevitable result. The more we depart from our own ideal of a perfect human, the more we become an idiot ourselves. The more we hate, the deeper we sink.

New communities

New visions for communities are needed, reinventing new forms of cooperation in societies. For example, instead of feeling at home in a country being based on ancestry, we could base it on participation in society. Create networks and campaigns with freelancers and employees to secure a fair working environment and rates. Or start feeling responsible for other children and elderly people in our extended social circle. This would enrich everyone's lives.

Open discussion

I think we need to have open discussions about democracy: the best guarantee for a healthy democracy is educated, organised and connected citizens. Elections are the least interesting aspect of democracy. What happens to me when I notice that people around you do not trust me? We can refuse to accept the opinion of someone but we should always accept the person themselves. We should really listen and not immediately reject and ignore. And continuously reflect on our own opinion. Everybody has an intuition of what is right or wrong. The more you trust and ask people about their opinion, the more people want to be part of the solution. And we should ask ourselves: do I not trust others or do I not trust myself?

Safe rooms: crossing mental borders

I think we need to create forums that allow us to change each other's minds: resolving conflicts, questioning enemy images. Spaces that are open for us to change our minds about what we once thought was right. To be aware that others think differently on the same issue. To question our certainty of our opinions.

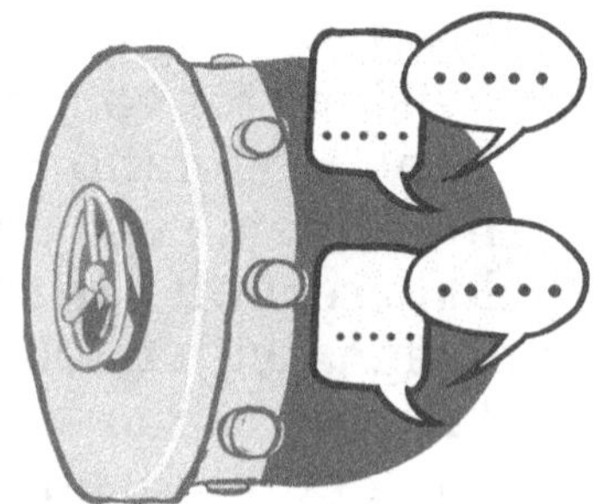

Opinions are like the opening at the end of the alimentary canal: everybody has one

How can we agree on anything when we are encouraged to disagree on everything? Members of a group who share the same views tend to become more extreme in those views. The people most likely to filter out opposing views are the ones who most need to hear them. It makes sense to examine ours every once in a while: when too many people are too certain about what they think, the polarisation between opinions is fostering rather than undermining extremists. The idea that you just have to put enough experts in one room and you will find a solution for any problem does not match reality: psychological safety is even more important.

Only when we feel safe we can really discuss

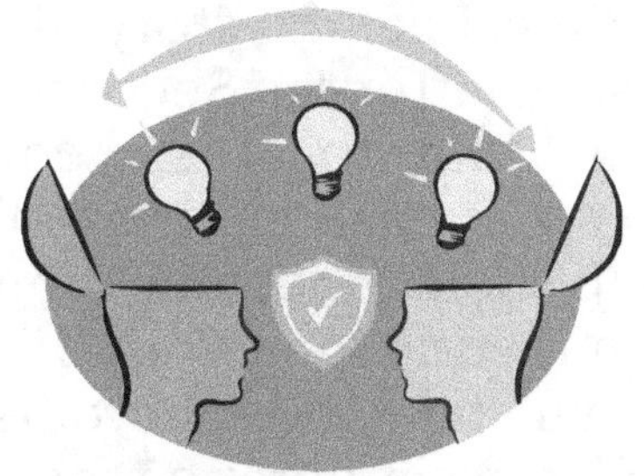

Google's Project Aristotle was a study conducted to identify the key factors that make a successful team. Google found that psychological safety was the linchpin of the five factors that impact team effectiveness:

- Psychological safety: individuals need safe space to take risks and make mistakes without fear of recriminations.

- Dependability: the team needs to ensure that work is done on time, and to a high standard.

- Structure and clarity: clear roles, plans and goals are essential.

-Meaning: work should be personally important to each one of us.

-Impact: people need to know that what they do matters and creates change.

Accepting truths

Discussions reach their limits when it comes to physical laws, observations of nature's principles and scientific facts. An outcome proven by millions of experiments will not be changed by a philosophical discussion. Engineers, scientists and experienced professionals should play a more significant role in public debate.

New narratives are needed

To confront the extremist narratives we need plausible, compassionate stories with a happy ending. Like the story of the generation after the Second World War: "Draw together a community that has fought together, to help society become more equal, eliminating long-standing racial, social and gender borders." Or: "Saving the planet from the collective ignorance that we are independent and disconnected from it."

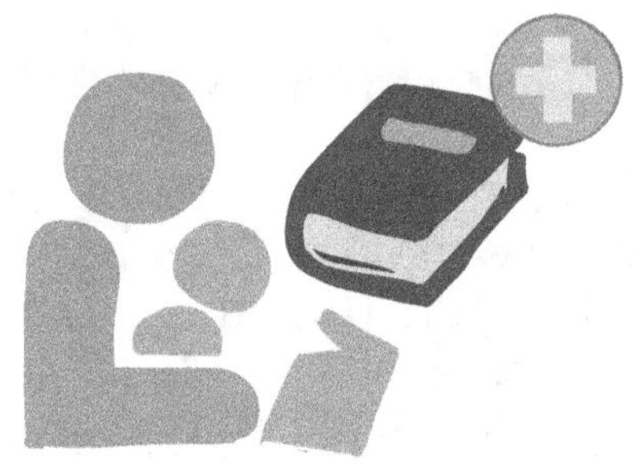

Preventing extremism and conspiracy theories

What we can do

-Do not patronise conspiracy theorists, but take their questions seriously. Remember, we are (modest) conspiracy theorists, too!

-Try to solve conflict together with compassion

-Aim to listen, to learn, to work together

-Help gain trust in science, institutions, and common sense

-Sustained personal engagement can change minds

-Provide people with facts

-Go in with consistent, strong counter-arguments

-Teach others and yourself to think critically about information and say, "I could be exposed to misinformation, so I'm going to be on the lookout for it." This will help us resist it when we encounter it next time.

-Find a common ground first: discuss for example why some people think the Earth is flat. (unless they think the earth is flat)

-Acknowledge that the other person, just like you, has the potential to become a better person: more wise, compassionate and patient

6.3 Creating the technological infrastructure for change

What is true for me?

Verifying information is essential today, where misinformation and disinformation can spread rapidly. Here are some techniques and strategies to help verify information:

Check multiple sources: Cross-reference the information across numerous reputable sources. If the same information is reported consistently across various sources, it's more likely to be accurate.

Use fact-checking websites: Websites like Snopes, Fact-Check.org, and PolitiFact specialize in fact-checking and debunking misinformation. They can help verify the accuracy of claims and stories.

Evaluate the source: Consider the credibility of the source. Reliable sources typically have a history of accurate reporting and are transparent about their journalistic standards. Be cautious of sources with a history of spreading misinformation or bias.

Check dates and context: Ensure that the information is current and hasn't been taken out of context. Sometimes old or outdated information resurfaces, leading to misunderstandings.

Examine supporting evidence: Look for supporting evidence such as quotes, data, or images to corroborate the information. Lack of supporting evidence or reliance on anonymous sources can be red flags.

Verify images and videos: Use reverse image search tools like Google Images or TinEye to verify the authenticity of images. For videos, analyse the content for signs of manipulation or editing.

Consult experts: When dealing with complex or technical information, consult experts in the relevant field to validate the accuracy of the information.

Be sceptical of unverified claims: Approach unverified claims with scepticism, especially if they seem sensational or too good to be true. It's better to withhold judgement until the information can be verified.

Consider biases: Be aware of your own biases and how they might influence your evaluation of information. Strive to approach information with an open mind and a critical eye.

Corroborate with primary sources: Whenever possible, refer to primary sources such as official documents, statements from original sources, or data from reputable organisations.

Follow trusted journalists and experts: Identify journalists and experts who consistently provide reliable information in areas of interest to you. Following them can help you stay informed and discern credible information from noise.

Stay informed about misinformation tactics: Educate yourself about common tactics used to spread misinformation, such as clickbait headlines, selective editing, and the use of false experts.

By employing these techniques and strategies, you can become a more discerning consumer of information and help combat the spread of misinformation.

And listen to your "inner wisdom". Sometimes you just know that something is a lie.

A counter network of information: educate and connect to organise change

Supporters of democracy need to unify and organise, forming groups locally, nationally, and internationally. They should use existing governmental and non-governmental organisations and networks. They should also organize teach-ins, voluntary programs, and extracurricular programs in schools and

universities. The power of truth is so strong that it overcomes the power of propaganda.

The wisdom of the cloud

Billions of complex, intelligent human minds respond to changes in a market, democracy, or society much better than a small group of planners. Planners do much damage. Maybe it's good to experiment with the decision

processes using the "wisdom of the cloud." I think we need well-designed decision processes that use a diversity of intelligence instead of one strong leader.

Decentralised content distribution powers a global "makers" movement

The goal of any corporation or privileged group is to control and monetise content creation, content distribution and consumption: Apple content on an Apple playback device, bought from the Apple content shop. Web 3 is bringing decentralised platforms and creator ownership of digital assets. And with this comes a diversity of voices.

114

"The global maker movement, which is seeing independent creators become a force in every industry as never before, is the most important movement of our time, and will have transformative political, sociological and economic consequences."

Orna Ross

Your personal editor is an algorithm

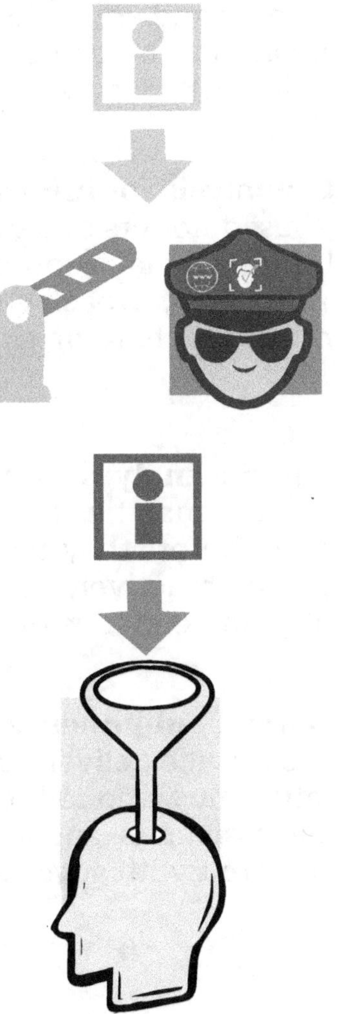

Whenever you click 'Like', browse a web page or buy something on Amazon you are programming how a web browser displays the world to you. It is all about the big question: what stuff are you tempted to buy? This filter will not help you see the world from other people's perspective. It will just display stories that reinforce your beliefs. Search results are dependent on the computer you're using and where you live. The army of trolls also distorts your web browser's reality. False, sensational stories get the most clicks. And make you see the world through the eyes of a troll.

Integrating artificial intelligence (AI) into democracy to enhance various aspects of governance, citizen participation, and decision-making processes. It's essential to approach the integration of AI in democracy with a focus on ethical considerations, transparency, and accountability to ensure that these technologies con-tribute positively to democratic values and principles. Public awareness and education are crucial to building trust in AI applications and democratic processes. Here are several ways in which AI could be integrated into democracy:

Data analysis for informed policy-making: AI can analyse vast amounts of data to provide policymakers with insights into social, economic, and environmental trends. This data-driven approach can facilitate evidence-based decision-making, helping governments formulate more effective policies.

Predictive analytics for risk assessment: AI can be used for predictive analytics to identify potential risks, challenges, or crises before they escalate. This capability allows governments to proactively address issues, allocate resources efficiently, and enhance overall crisis management.

Enhanced public services: AI technologies can optimise public service delivery by automating routine tasks, improving efficiency, and reducing bureaucratic delays. Chatbots, virtual assistants, and automated systems can enhance citizen interactions with government services.

Citizen engagement and participation: AI-powered platforms can promote greater citizen engagement by providing interactive tools for participation in decision-making processes. These platforms can gather public opinions, feedback, and suggestions, enabling a more inclusive and participatory democracy.

Election integrity and security: AI can contribute to election security by detecting and preventing potential threats such as disinformation campaigns, cyberattacks, and voter fraud. Machine learning algorithms can analyse patterns to identify and mitigate risks.

Personalised information and communication: AI algorithms can help tailor information to individual citizens' preferences and needs, providing personalised updates on government activities, policies, and civic engagement opportunities. This can enhance communication between the government and citizens.

Accessibility and inclusivity: AI technologies can improve accessibility for citizens with disabilities, ensuring that government services and information are available to all. For example, AI-driven tools can assist individuals with visual or hearing impairments navigate digital platforms.

Smart infrastructure and urban planning: AI can contribute to innovative city initiatives by optimising urban planning, transportation systems, and infrastructure management. This can lead to more sustainable, efficient, and citizen-friendly urban environments.

Enhanced decision support systems: AI can assist policymakers by providing sophisticated decision support systems that analyse complex scenarios, simulate outcomes, and help evaluate the potential impacts of different policy options.

Ethical AI governance: Establishing ethical guidelines and governance frameworks for the use of AI in democracy is crucial. This includes ensuring AI systems' transparency, fairness, and accountability to prevent biases and protect individual rights.

AI in law enforcement and judicial processes: AI can be employed in law enforcement for crime prediction and analysis and in judicial processes for legal research and case analysis. However, careful attention must be paid to bias and fairness issues in these applications.

Cybersecurity and privacy protection: AI can enhance cybersecurity measures to protect critical infrastructure and citizens' data. Additionally, AI tools can help monitor and enforce privacy regulations to safeguard individual rights.

What do you think?

Will AI dehumanise processes and reduce human cooperative interactions?

Information is king

It is a challenge to bring people more than one side of the story. Using an uncensored internet to disseminate information allows people to inform themselves at very little cost. They then can develop public opinion movements against or of supporting an issue. This allows for diverse viewpoints and creates an awareness of the diversity of perspectives on a single issue. Well-informed participants are better able to contribute to the deliberation process, and this is likely to lead to better outcomes. Ordinary citizens can build themselves up into influential political commentators. They can voice criticism that traditional media would never dare, pushing the limits of press freedom. Social media are a democratising platform to elevate the voices of the oppressed and opposition statistics but they are also increasingly responsible for the spread of fake news and smear campaigns. Digital fact-checking and troll-spotting software and methods need to be improved.

The "wise AI guardian"?

We are already comfortable with AI systems taking our lives in their "hands" in many parts. Although they appear to be objective, any AI starts with a human programmer and a powerful investor: a huge corporation or a privileged group.

What do you think?

Would an advanced intelligent artificial agent make better decisions to maximise society's benefit than a group of people?

Are human decisions irrational and inefficient by comparison?

What consequences will this have for our social and democratic order?

Who will take the responsibility when things go wrong?

Interesting quote

"As algorithms push humans out of the job market, wealth and power might become concentrated in the hands of the tiny elite that owns the all powerful algorithms, creating unprecedented social and political inequality. Today millions of taxi drivers, bus drivers and truck drivers have significant economic and political clout, each commanding a tiny share of the transportation market. If their collective interests are threatened, they can unionise, go on strike, stage boycotts and create powerful voting blocks. However, once millions of human drivers are replaced by a single algorithm, all that wealth and power will be cornered by the corporation that owns the algorithm, and by the handful of billionaires who own the corporation."

"... the algorithms might themselves become the owners. Human law already recognises intersubjective entities like corporations and nations as 'legal persons'. Though Toyota or Argentina has neither a body nor a mind, they are subject to international laws, they can own land and money, and they can sue and be sued in court."

Yuval Noah Harari

Data-driven democracy?

In one way data shows us as we are, not as we think we are. By gathering together and synthesising large amounts of real-time data – giving equal consideration to everyone's interests, preferences, and values – we could create the sharpest and fullest possible portrait of the common good. Un-

der this model, policy could be based on an incomparably rich and accurate picture of our lives: what we do, what we need, what we think, what we say, how we feel. It would, in theory, ensure a more significant measure of political equality – as it would be drawn from everyone equally, not just those who tend to get involved in the political process.

Voting apps

The financial and border security sectors already use reliable technology to identify individuals. This technology could simplify the voting process and shift democracy from a "wise elite" model to a "deliberation model." This might even encourage apathetic and disillusioned voters to take a more active role. AI could be made subject to the ethics of its human masters, helping to draft and amend legislation. It could play a part in democracy while remaining subordinate to traditional democratic processes like human deliberation and votes.

Interesting facts

In an opinion poll taken after the 2015 general election, 65 percent of people who didn't vote said they would be more likely to if the ballot was somewhere more convenient, such as a supermarket or an office.

Four out of ten people said they would be more likely to vote if they could do it online. Brazil, Belgium, the Philippines, India and the US have all used e-voting in one form or another.

Independent currencies and the dangers of a cashless society

In a cash-based transaction, the control over the money exchange lies between the seller and the buyer. However, in a cashless society, the privileged group overseeing the cashless infrastructure can approve or decline these exchanges. They can halt money flow or impose conditions if a buyer or seller doesn't meet their criteria. These privileged groups also possess access to citizens' financial information, making negative

interest rates and the risk of total loss possible if the group's bank goes bankrupt or is compromised by hacking. Anonymously conducting payments is no longer feasible, as each transaction is traced.

The pros of an "independent" currency

Digital currencies like Bitcoin operate without central authority control. Any citizen with internet access and a digital wallet holds complete ownership and control over their funds, eliminating the necessity for third-party intermediaries. Cryptocurrencies use highly secure, cost-effective methods to safeguard transactions. Transactions are transparent, publicly recorded, and maintain a detailed transaction history in a "blockchain." The tracking of individuals involved in NFT (non-fungible token) transactions depends on the blockchain's level of anonymity and privacy features. Generally, blockchain transactions are pseudonymous, meaning users are identified by alphanumeric addresses rather than personal information. However, suppose someone links their real identity to their blockchain address or uses a platform with Know Your Customer (KYC) requirements. In that case, authorities may trace transactions back to individuals if someone links their real identity to their blockchain address or uses a platform with Know Your Customer

(KYC) requirements. It's essential to be aware of the privacy features or lack thereof on the specific blockchain or platform used for NFT transactions. Time will tell if digital currencies can serve as a store of value to guard against devaluation, offering potential for substantial returns. Additionally, they are difficult to be blocked, making them a tool for promoting economic freedom.

The cons of an "independent" currency

Digital currencies can experience rapid and substantial value fluctuations. Once transactions are made, they are irreversible. Network congestion may result in slower transaction processing. Proof of work (PoW) mining demands considerable energy, raising environmental concerns. PoW  is a consensus algorithm used in blockchain networks. In a PoW system, participants (often called miners) solve complex mathematical problems to validate and add new transactions to the blockchain. The first participant to solve the problem gets the right to add a new block and is rewarded with newly created cryptocurrency coins.

PoW serves as a security mechanism, requiring computational effort to add blocks. This makes it difficult for malicious actors to manipulate the blockchain. The first and most well-known cryptocurrency, Bitcoin uses PoW as its consensus algorithm.

Additionally, privileged groups may resist the integration of digital currencies into the conventional financial system, potentially impeding their universal acceptance as a form of payment. When we deposit our money in a traditional bank we can align our moral values with the credit policies of the bank, preventing our money from being used for loans to environmentally damaging companies for example.

Cryptocurrencies as financial security and pension funds?

The younger generation often spends more than 50% of their monthly income on rent. Traditional financial assets are expensive, and the price of tangible assets like real estate keeps going up, and many can afford much less than they do every year. Cryptocurrencies are available to everybody.

This might give ordinary people an opportunity to save for their pension.

What do you think?

Would you mind if everybody knew how many hours per day you played games last month?

Do everybody know exactly what you spend your money on?

We are already comfortable with AI systems taking our lives in their "hands" in many parts of our lives. Would an advanced intelligent artificial agent make better decisions to maximise the benefit for society than a group of people?

Are human decisions irrational and inefficient by comparison?

What consequences will this have for our social and democratic order?

Who will take the responsibility when things go wrong?

6.4 Creating new decision-making processes

Citizens' assemblies

Politicians are frustrated because they often went into politics to change the world but their hands are tied by the reality of party politics and political culture in general. And once the election cam-paign is over there are still groups with different opinions on any subject within a political party. For voters, the big disappointment with politicians is that their priority is to cling to power instead of solving actual problems. Due to conflicts of interest and entrenched tribal loyalties, democratic institutions can frequently become mired in impasses. Just like in a big cooperation, politicians of all parties work together, moderated by an external, unbiased moderator. The role of an impartial moderator would be to ensure that the forum remains a constructive and inclusive space for participants to express diverse opinions and engage in meaningful dialogue. An favour an impartial moderator and does not favour any particular viewpoint, group, or individual. They strive to remain neutral and personal from avoiding promoting their personal avoid promoting their opinions or biases. The moderator treats all participants equally, enforces forum rules, keeps an open mind, and is receptive to diverse perspectives. When conflicts arise, an unbiased moderator intervenes impartially, striving to find resolutions that align with the forum's guidelines and principles, communicating openly with forum participants, and providing clear explanations for decisions and actions taken. Transparency builds trust and helps participants understand the reasoning behind moderation choices, addressing concerns, questions, or feedback promptly in a timely manner. This accessibility contributes to a sense of accountability and community within the forum.

In such circumstances, the government could have the option to appoint committees to establish a citizen assembly. A citizen assembly can offer resolutions to societal or political challenges by involving the public, with the assistance of experts, in a process that encompasses small group deliberations, extensive debates, and a sequence of voting procedures. The randomness of choice of the members of the citizens' assembly leaves party politics outside the discussion.

ICT components

ICT can assist democracy only when all the following components are present:

- -Access information (LISTEN): people must be able
  to educate themselves on what the government is
  doing that may affect them.

- -Send information (SPEAK UP): a channel to gather
  the suggestions of the people.

- -Allow suggestions to be understood (BE HEARD): the
  government must be able to process all suggestions
  sent, no matter the volume.

- -Get an answer (ACKNOWLEDGEMENT): the population must trust they will be heard.

- -Verify suggestion status (ACTUAL PARTICIPATION):
  the population must be informed of what will be
  done about their suggestions. Citizens derive a
  meaningful sense of satisfaction from having con-
  tributed to the decision-making process.

Non-commercial discussion forums

Democracy needs a forum for discussion, not a marketplace. When
a discussion forum transforms
into a hub for misinformation and
hate, it poses a risk to fact-based
decision-making and the value
of truth itself. The casualty will
be the truth if content is framed
and prioritised solely based on

its ability to generate advertising revenue. The "community guidelines" of social media platforms are not impartial; they are crafted to serve the interests of shareholders rather than fostering a space for free-thinking and uncensored expression. When the discourse space is predominantly controlled by those with the power to censor or unleash an army of propaganda bots, the conversation is distorted in favour of those with superior technology, not necessarily superior ideas.

Community land trusts

A community land trust (CLT) is a non-profit organisation established to act as a custodian of land on behalf of a specific local community. It plays a crucial role as a long-term guardian for affordable housing, community gardens, civic structures, commercial areas, and oth-

er community assets in the service of that community. CLTs aim to strike a balance between the interests of individuals seeking secure land tenure for housing and land use and the broader community, with the goal of fulfilling a range of social objectives.

Forming assemblies

The main components of a multinational society need to be represented and to act as authentic constituent actors. Here's a suggestion for an international assembly:

- -25% randomly drawn among the entire body of citizens

-25% directly elected by the citizens via transnational lists

-25% representing member-state governments

-25% represent territories and municipalities.

Promoting voting

Most countries have a voter turnout of less than 60%. We need to make it easy and reliable to register and cast votes. But most of all, we need to raise awareness of the importance of voting. 

6.5 Creating new ethical, economical models

Mixed and social economies work.

Looking back in history, a mixed economy seems to have worked best: big corporations, transport, the internet, infrastructure, and education are controlled by the public, while farms and small businesses face fewer regulations. In a social market economy, the business company is relatively free, while the state provides  universal health care, free education, and generous unemployment benefits.

Self-management instead of shareholders

When the employees are shareholders, they solve problems themselves instead of just doing the minimum. They are also protected from corporate criminals raiding their pension funds.

Interesting facts

An unfortunate example of a pension fund raid happened in November 2020 in the UK. Arcadia Group, owned by Sir Philip Green, went into administration, a form of bankruptcy protection in the United Kingdom. One significant issue during Arcadia's financial troubles was the deficit in its pension funds. This was after Sir Philip Green paid himself a dividend of £1.2bn. The pensioners relying on those funds for their retirement income got nothing to retire on.

Improving working conditions

Regular independent investigations into working conditions, ethical labels for products, unions and laws securing best practices, tax rates and wages can protect workers from criminal entrepreneurs.

New ways for banking

Banks could focus on being sustainable and their environmental, cultural and social impact. They should allow customers an insight into their business and inform them about the projects and businesses that they invest in.

There should be a public debate about sustainable, ethical best practices for all of these groups. Can we imagine a society driven by compassion, intelligence, collaboration, skills and universal responsibility instead of debt and profit?

"New deal" program for the planet

The planet could use something like Roosevelt's "New Deal" program, which aligned public incentives with public interests.

Roosevelt's New Deal refers to a series of programs and policies implemented by US President Franklin D. Roosevelt during the 1930s in response to the Great Depression. The New Deal aimed to address the economic challenges and to relieve the American people during one of the most severe economic downturns in US history. The New Deal was a significant departure from previous policies, which left the economy unregulated, as it marked a more active role for the federal government in addressing economic challenges and promoting social welfare. While it faced criticism from some quarters, the New Deal is generally credited with helping to stabilise the economy and providing relief to millions of Americans during unprecedented economic hardship. It strengthened public power to counterbalance private power. It included progressive taxation, taking more tax the more people earn, and stopping big corporations from splitting into smaller units to avoid tax.

A new version should also include policies to ensure the highest-paid receive no more than ten times the salary of those at the bottom of the pay scale and eliminate loopholes for big corporations to avoid paying their taxes.

Progressive taxation

...means taking more tax the more people earn.

Income: 1000.00

Income left after tax: 1000.00

Income: 200, 000.00

The income left after tax: 52 000.00

Income: 1, 000, 000.00

The income left after tax: 161 000.00

The money earned from these taxes can be spent on social security and unemployment insurance. Indirectly, it gives us purchasing power that will keep the economy booming.

Universal basic income (UBI)

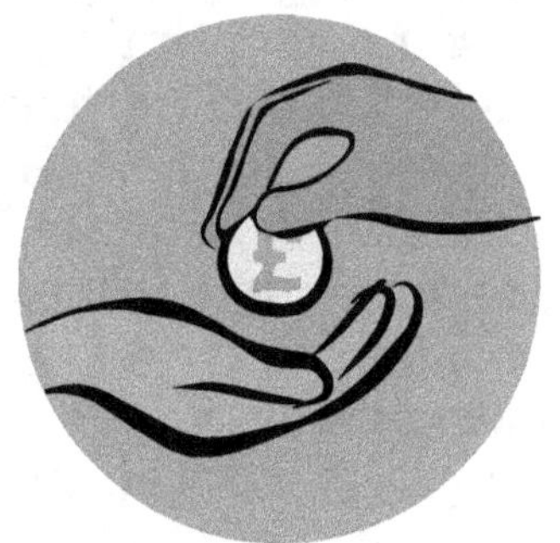

A **means test** is a method used to determine eligibility for receiving financial assistance or benefits based on an individual's or household's ,economic situation. It assesses an individual's income, assets, and sometimes other factors like household size or expenses to determine whether they qualify for assistance programs. Means tests are commonly used in various government programs, such as social welfare benefits, healthcare subsidies, student financial aid, and housing assistance. A means test aims to ensure that limited resources are allocated to those who need them the most while preventing abuse or misuse of public funds by individuals who have sufficient means to support themselves.

Universal basic income takes a different approach: it is a social welfare proposal in which all citizens of a given population regularly receive a minimum income through an unconditional transfer payment, i.e., without a means test or need to work.

Potential pros of UBI:

-Empowering important traditionally unpaid roles for non-working parents and caregivers

-Preventing employees from taking low-income jobs

-Allows citizens who need to train/study/retrain or focus on learning

-Improves physical and mental health

-Reduces poverty and income inequality

-Makes leaving an abusive partner easier from a financial point of view

-Will continuously stimulate the economy, as UBI recipients get money to spend

-Saves money by closing down government administration dealing with poverty

-In a society where robots perform most tasks, ensuring wealth is redistributed to everybody.

Potential cons of UBI:

-UBI is expensive and removes the incentive to work, adversely affecting the economy and leading to a labor and skills shortage

-Earned income motivates people to work, be successful, work cooperatively with colleagues, and gain skills.

The modern economy requires collective action.

The modern economy needs a government to invest in infrastructure, education, technology, primary research, and education. significant new technologies started with taxpayers' funding: the army researched new technologies. The GPS and touch screens used in phones. Google's search engine algorithm is partly based on a National Science Foundation innovation.

Artists' work is used without compensation for profit-making AI services. The profits created through technologies should flow back to citizens.

Volunteering

We could encourage a society where volunteers trying to ischarity improve it are supported and acknowledged more—making a difference by teaching art and music, helping older people, cleaning up local parks, working for an animal charity, or staffing a food bank.

7. Education and the arts

7.1 Privileged groups abuse education

Education scares privileged groups.

Privileged groups only allow democracy and liberty as long as it doesn't threaten their wealth and power. Students can play around while studying; they become obedient individuals upon graduation. Educational institutions are closely monitored; if there is a danger to wealth and power, an "alarm" goes off.

Deprivation, hiding and falsification of information

Books of the past allow us to accumulate knowledge instead of relearning. When insights into the workings of repression, exploitation, and resistance are deleted or altered, we can have little understanding of how power works. Information is only created, presented, and disseminated for economic gain, which threatens democratic processes and public goods.

Education promotes, sustains, and maintains the privileges of privileged groups.

Is the educational system resistant to knowledge because it is dominated by money and power? Trustees, often people with connections to privileged groups, control universities and will make sure dissidence becomes a danger. The educational system is not an oasis within society but a reflection of the dominant power structures. Additionally, humanitarian organisations and sciences are financially backed by privileged groups to further their agendas, shaping pre-defined consent. An indoctrination process that imposes a wilful blindness.

Questions like: 'Will this knowledge enable our sponsors to increase production and profits? Will it produce economic growth?' are dominating some Universities.

Interest in keeping privileges instead of teaching enlightenment

The more familiar individuals become with an organisation, like a school or a public organisation, the more interest they have in the system that provides them with privileges. Middle-class teachers worried about their safety. Public servants and their working hours. Out of interest in keeping their privileges, some teachers teach justification and legitimization of what would be otherwise considered inhumane, exploitative, and oppressive. Or they become so unprofessional over time that their teachings could be of better quality. Or it's just wrong. Our education system doesn't encourage dissent and critical thinking.

Lots of money, still failures: schools as containment centres for disposable pupils

All the wealth, technology and huge number of courses and universities still produce "educational failures." The educational system is not designed to educate those who are struggling. Uneducated people with no resources and no future opportunities become dysfunctional people in society.

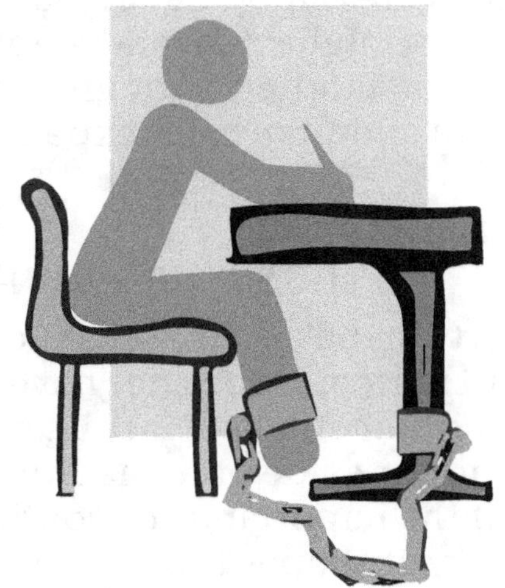

7.2 The potential of schools

There are no simple, universal answers.

Schools should teach pupils ideals and analytical tools to help them form their own opinions. This includes studying history from multiple perspectives and learning about people who are questioning the system. Knowledge and wisdom should not be static but constantly examining, forming and revising opinions.

Awareness coupled with actions

The classroom should be a place where students learn about the world and how to make a difference in it. It should not be a place where they are isolated from the world or taught to criticise the world without trying to change it. A place to learn about history and culture, where people are free to express their opinions, even if they are unpopular. A place to develop intellectual and emotional understanding through compassion and first-hand experience.

7.3 The arts and democracy

Those who control art control society

Art can be an instrument of war. True art is free; it does not have to please, and sometimes it inspires us to look at the dark side of humanity. It reminds us of the importance of conflict in democracy. It shapes how we see our world,

a hammer with which to shape reality. It helps us imagine a better, more beautiful world – a more important job than the president has got. Art is a necessary instrument for human happiness.

Ideas are unstoppable

Bombing, censoring, distorting: repressing ideas strengthens them, creating even more like-minded ideas. Ideas mean a different world can exist. Looking at the world through somebody else's ideas can make us empathetic. Art can fill dry, uninteresting ideas with equalize material and military power; that's why it plays an important role in activism. It can mobilise people, bringing suggestions and demands to the attention of the citizens, without having power of the press.

8. Anti-corruption strategies

Secure transparency

Transparency is the oxygen of democracy: the principle of self-government is meaningless if citizens cannot see how they are governed. Using modern technology, all important government meetings and voting should be available for all citizens. Democracy requires an informed citizenry, as information engenders trust and control over politicians to serve the electorate's desires.

An effective alliance is formed when citizens collaborate: the political opposition, cultural leaders, idealists, religious communities, unions, and NGOs. Connect radicalism, labour movements and education. The independent media can motivate everybody else by reminding them of what they might lose: the planet

they live on. Democracy and structure are essential to the success of every movement. There has to be fairness in the way we operate. Within any organisation we have to agree on an internal structure of rules of how we operate, what our version of democracy looks like.

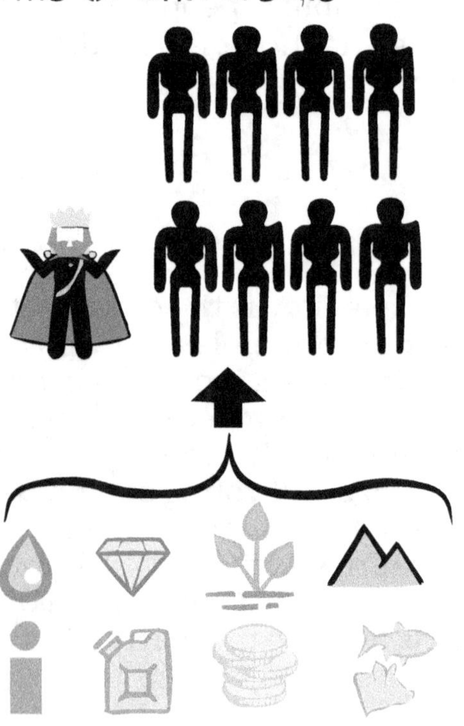

Such a coalition should agree on criteria for fairness and integrity in public life and make them part of a common program. If one or more political parties adopt the criteria they should be given credit for their efforts.

Corrupters excluded

Anti-corruption strategies that are implemented by and in co-operation with the corrupters themselves are bound to fail.

Creating registries

A registry of institutional decision-making people should be created, making public:

- The financial interests of all members of parliament

- Government officials and their close family

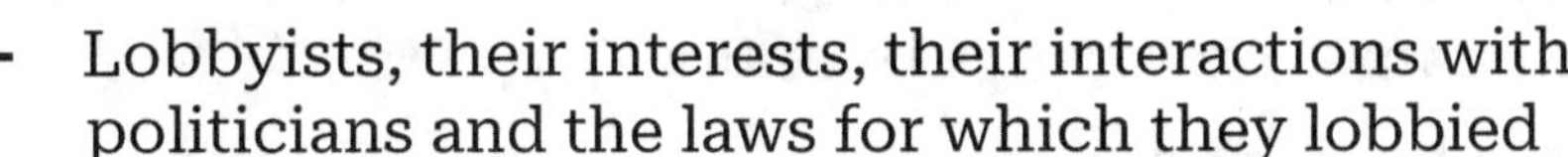

- Lobbyists, their interests, their interactions with politicians and the laws for which they lobbied

- Companies, trusts and foundations benefiting from particular laws

- Deals and agreements between companies and the government.

An independent body needs the powers and resources to investigate any malpractice or corruption, also on an international level.

Incentives for privileged groups

Create incentives for privileged groups to "go clean". Such as a reduced prison sentence or even no sentence at all. On top of this, reformed criminals would be reintegrated in society as they have done their redemption. These incentives are provided by close public mon-itoring and disclosure. Using the institutional weapons at hand, the coalition should try to unseat the privileged groups in politics or the professions by creating disclosure campaigns, trying to end their monopoly of influence. This makes it easier to reintegrate former culprits into society.

Taking responsibility

Public contracts can't be issued to companies operating out of tax havens. No arms and technology can be sold to countries abusing human rights.

Dangers of technology

Technology is not neutral. We must be vigilant of the individuals implementing it and have independent control mechanisms. A lack of opacity and complexity is often good for people who want to use them for personal rather than public gain.

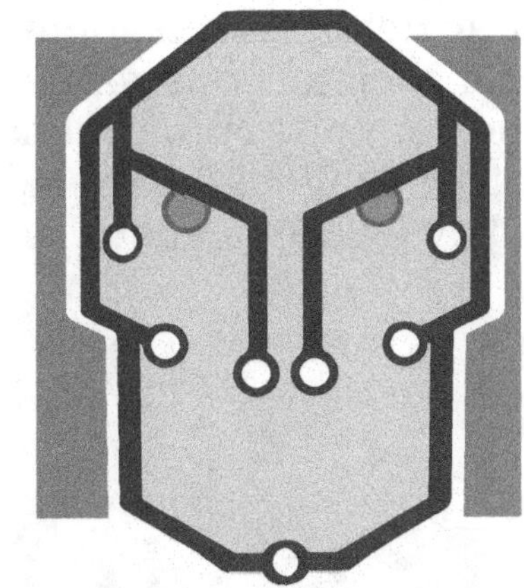

Take the health sector for example: algorithms already make the most important decisions of our lives for us. We are coming to a point where the algorithm knows us better than we know ourselves. What if the algorithm makes fewer mistakes? Are we happy to give up the authority over our lives? Maybe we'll reach a point when we face certain death if we disconnect from the algorithm? It is likely that the privileged groups will get a health upgrade much earlier than everybody else. Over time this may even lead to two completely different biological species.

Interesting fact

The film "Gattaca" (1997) is a science fiction drama set in a future society where genetic engineering determines one's social and professional status. The story follows Vincent Freeman, who was conceived naturally and is considered genetically inferior, or an "In-Valid." Despite his genetic limitations, Vincent dreams of becoming an astronaut. To achieve this, he assumes the identity of Jerome Morrow, a genetically superior individual who is paralyzed after a car accident. With Jerome's genetic material, Vincent gains entry into the Gattaca Aerospace Corporation.

As Vincent prepares for a mission to Titan, he faces increasing scrutiny when a murder investigation at Gattaca threatens to expose his true identity. Along the way, he forms a relationship with Irene Cassini, a fellow Gattaca employee with her own genetic imperfections. The film explores themes of genetic determinism, identity, and the triumph of human spirit over societal constraints. Ultimately, Vincent's determination and Jerome's support enable him to fulfil his dream of space travel, challenging the notion that one's fate is determined solely by their genetic makeup.

Interdependence

We all need each other or we are not going to survive: whether it's climate change, globalisation or robots doing all the work. We all have to live together: that's much easier in harmony with ourselves and nature. We HAVE to work together instead of competing with other organisations; we are building on their work and they are building on ours, collectively strengthening the cause.

Global boiling

In the next fifty years huge numbers of us will migrate from the inhabitable hot countries and the flooded coastlines to higher and cooler parts of the earth. The successful integration of these climate migrants will decide the future of all organised life on earth. Privileged groups are going to use these future challenges to gain even more power.

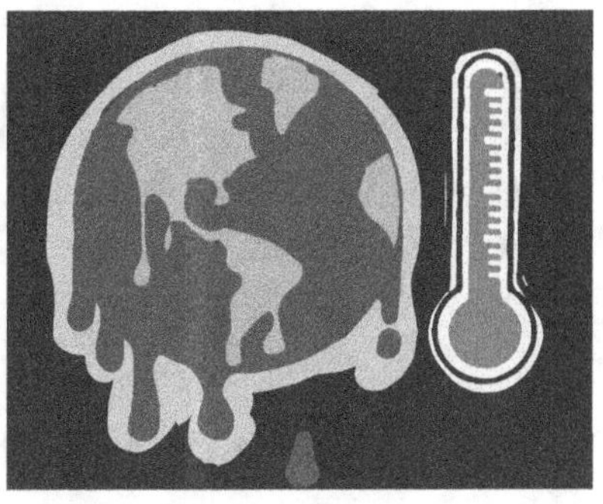

The privileged groups economy

Because they are not taxed appropriately, privileged groups have a lot of disposable money. This drives asset prices through the roof. Our parents could save for 10 years and buy a house. Today most of us need to save for 60 years to buy and finally own a place to live.

Robot workforce

We are progressing toward a society where robots, hardware, and software handle the majority of labour. To ensure these benefits are shared with everyone, one solution is to establish a public trust fund into which corporations allocate a portion of their shares. This mechanism could pave the way for a universal basic income that scales in tandem with automation.

The concept of work in the age of automation

A society of "no more workers" with free housing, food, and healthcare? These arrangements need a political will to materialise, otherwise only the privileged groups are going to profit.

What do you think?

An obligatory community service in exchange for a basic income? Can we help someone else get something for free, especially if they don't belong to our community? Can we handle the idea of being replaced? What is going to happen to us when the need for excessive work to fill our empty lives, to give them meaning and purpose, can't be fulfilled any longer?

Interesting quote

"What will they do all day? One answer might be drugs and computer games. Unnecessary people might spend increasing amounts of time within 3D virtual reality worlds, that would provide them with far more excitement and emotional engagement than the drab reality outside. Yet such a development would deal a mortal blow to the liberal belief in the sacredness of human life and of human experiences."

—Yuel Noah Harari

Our thoughts are no longer free

Today, some Chinese factory workers and train operators are compelled to wear brain-monitoring devices that assess their concentration levels and active brain areas. If the outcomes do not meet specific criteria, they face termination of their work contracts. This highlights

the need to discuss expanding the right to freedom of speech to encompass "freedom of thought."

What do you think?

Should we give up our freedom in exchange for efficient, data-driven public services owned and run by tech giants (privileged groups)?

10. Organising system change

Civil disobedience: timing the change

Changes to systems happen often during economic crises or other periods of societal stress. Civil disobedience is a willingness to decide when laws are consonant with morals. Laws are very often not an objective representation of democracy but rules made up by privileged groups. Redressing of serious grievances has been done very often by civil disobedience, not the state.

The pattern of lasting system change

The roads to the end of injustices like slavery, apartheid, the Berlin Wall or the English occupation of India have many similarities:

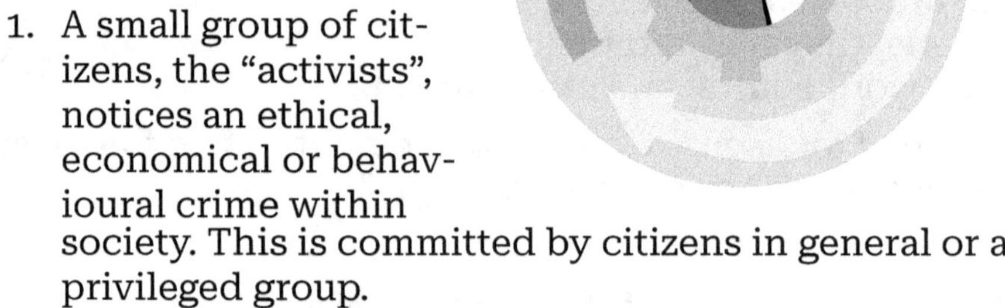

1. A small group of citizens, the "activists", notices an ethical, economical or behavioural crime within society. This is committed by citizens in general or a privileged group.

2. The activists start investigating, analysing and documenting the problem.

3. The activists campaign to inform and educate, using legal and illegal techniques.

4. Privileged groups try to prevent the campaign using various techniques, including violence.

5. The activists manage to convince existing networks to join their cause.

6. The campaign grows into a popular mass movement. The activists find parliamentary representation.

7. Parliament approves new laws and policies, making the crime illegal.

Revolution versus steady, gentle change

Revolutions aim at rapid progress, and leaders often gain legitimacy through charisma. They are less concerned with building institutions of accountability than with completing the takeover of the state from the previous rulers. The revolutionary spirit will fade, and it's that it is transformed into something worthwhile. Once a balance of power has been achieved among social groups through an organic and gradual process, universal rules and norms serve as significant constraints on privileged groups and their strategies within a given policy. Corruption does resurface, however, when accountability becomes weak or non-existent.

A motor for change: public social drama

"Brave underdogs go into battle against evil." Breaking the rules gets attention and shows that you are serious and unafraid. Imagine the grandma carried away in handcuffs, a doctor in jail, or a woman offering a flower who is hit with a baton. The social drama triggers citizens' unrest and, finally, change. Make sure it's well-documented and publicised.

1. You need 50 000 people (according to Extinction Rebellion co-founder Roger Hallam).

2. Go to the capital. That is where the government, elites, and the media are.

3. Break the law: sit down on roads; paint government buildings.

No cost nobody cares

Each day you block a city or infrastructure, the economic costs go up exponentially. After a week it's a national crisis.

It has to be fun

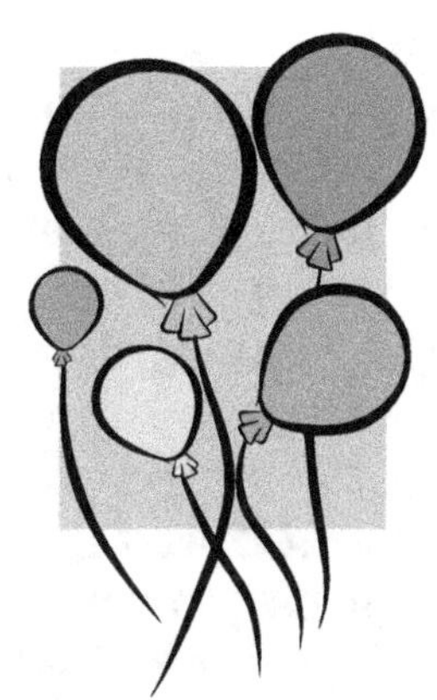

If we can't dance at it, it isn't a real revolution. A glimpse of what life could be. A world where we are selflessly treating each other kindly with no artificial distinctions. We can't afford infighting, claiming to stand for equality and fairness when the environment of the movements we create is toxic.

Change: no use using violence

Violence destroys democracy and the relationships with opponents, which are essential to creating peaceful outcomes in social conflict. It destroys the diversity and community basis upon which all successful mass mobilisations are based. The young, the old, and the vulnerable will leave the space. Violence almost always leads to fascism and authoritarianism. We need to train people not to get violent when provoked.

Interesting quote

"... when violence is used, the resolution that is achieved comes at the expense of people's human rights, safety, and security. The problem will not truly have been resolved but merely suppressed, and it will inevitably eventually resurface. History shows us that military victories and defeats are not lasting. This is also true in our lives, in the context of family and friends....."

HH The Dalai Lama

The logic of compassion

Reciprocity is a social norm of responding to a positive action with another positive action, rewarding kind actions and the community, and making it possible to build continuing relationships and exchanges. A democracy needs the foundations of reciprocity, moral obligation, duty toward the community, and trust. In this climate, individuals can even gradually transcend from reciprocity to giving with no expectation of future reward.

Government of the people of this village, by the people of this country, for the people of this planet

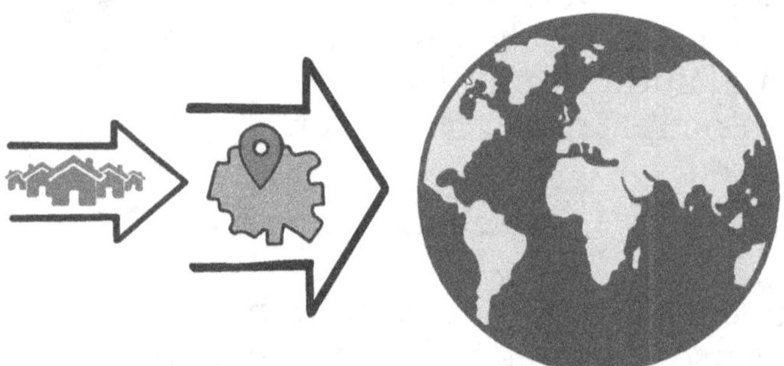

We want our children to be confident, Democrats, to go out and be part of the world and face its contradictions and conflicts. This way, we all become part of a conversation that is bigger than ourselves. I think we all need to play a part in promoting democratic values and fundamental freedoms throughout the world, transforming ungovernable areas on every continent into countries where the happiness of the citizens is a dominant policy.

In the end

I think our answers have to come from within ourselves, by developing a deep understanding of subjects such as cause and effect, interdependence and the reality of life's suffering. And cultivating compassion. A long, slow path to enlightenment. There isn't a way to speed things up. Apart from the motivation to lay the foundations to make our children's future a little bit happier.

Interesting quote

"... the potential for renewal exemplified by your generation is encircled by the shadows of the old world: a dark chaos of pain and tears. You must stand up to the wilful opposition to knowledge that is at large today, which is fraught with danger, where hatred, selfishness, violence, greed and fanaticism are threatening the very future of life on earth. I know that you have the persistence and strength to take on the future, and that you will succeed in drawing a line under the willed ignorance that you have inherit-ed.

My young friends, you are my hope for humanity."

HH The Dalai Lama

WE HAVE A SHARED VISION OF CHANGE

Creating a world that is fit for generations to come.

WE SET OUR MISSION ON WHAT IS NECESSARY

Mobilising 3.5% of the population to achieve system change – using ideas such as "Momentum-driven organising" to achieve this.

WE NEED A REGENERATIVE CULTURE

Creating a culture which is healthy, resilient and adaptable.

WE OPENLY CHALLENGE OURSELVES AND OUR TOXIC SYSTEM

Leaving our comfort zones to take action for change.

WE VALUE REFLECTING AND LEARNING

Following a cycle of action, reflection, learning, and planning for more action.

Learning from other movements and contexts as well as our own experiences.

WE WELCOME EVERYONE AND EVERY PART OF EVERYONE

Working actively to create safer and more accessible spaces.

WE ACTIVELY MITIGATE FOR POWER

Breaking down hierarchies of power for more equitable participation.

WE AVOID BLAMING AND SHAMING.

We live in a toxic system, but no one individual is to blame.

WE ARE A NON-VIOLENT NETWORK

Using non-violent strategy and tactics as the most effective way to bring about change.

WE ARE BASED ON AUTONOMY AND DECENTRALISATION

We collectively create the structures we need to challenge power.

Sources & inspiration

Development editing: Andrew Chapman/ **preparetopublish. com**

Additional proofreading : KestanWritersSolutions

Beta Readers: Claire Brooks, John Newton, Guy Ramage, Dionne Maynes

EPUB formatting: Amber Yusuf

THANK YOU:

JON BAIRD

ROSEMARY BECHLER

RICHARD BLANEY

COLIN DAGGIT

ROSEMARIE JELEN

1. Attack on "old school democracy"

Inspired by articles and information on Wikipedia and **www.**

2. Recognising dictatorship

Inspired by articles and information on the Peterson Institute for International Economics (PIIE).

3. Controlling everybody

Inspired by the work of Prof Dr Rainer Mausfeld.

4. Information and psychological control techniques

Inspired by the work of Prof Dr Rainer Mausfeld and the book *Economix* by Michael Goodwin, illustrated by Dan E. Burr.

5. Using extremism to stay in power

Inspired by the articles and talks of Fintan o'Toole, Yanis Varoufakis and Diem 25.

6. Ideas for a backbone democracy

Inspired by *Art Matters* by Neil Gaiman and Chris Riddell; HH the Dalai Lama' "How AI could kill off democracy", Jamie Bartlett; *Future Politics* by Jamie Susskind; "Who needs democracy when you have data?", Christina Larson; "Technology as a new backbone to democracy" by Ana Cristina Bicharra Garcia, A. C. B. Garcia, Fernando B. Pinto, Neves Inhaúma and Inhaúma Neves Ferraz.

7. Upcoming challenges

Inspired by Yanis Varoufakis, Richard Blaney and Diem 25.

10. Organising system change

Inspired by Roger Halham, the Dalai Lama's book *A Call for Revolution* and Howard Zinn on Democratic Education.

Links

www.un.org/en/about-us/un-charter/full-text

www.ipsos.com/en-uk/political-monitor-archive